A Relational Hermeneutic of Kindness

Dwayne Cole

Parson's Porch Books
www.parsonsporchbooks.com

A Relational Hermeneutic of Kindness
ISBN: Softcover 978-1-949888-61-4
Copyright © 2019 by Dwayne Cole

All rights reserved. No part of this book may be reproduced or transmitted in any form or by any means, electronic or mechanical, including photocopying, recording, or by any information storage and retrieval system, without permission in writing from the publisher.

A Relational Hermeneutic of Kindness

Contents

Preface	7
Introduction	11
God as Relational Kindness	14
Jesus Self-Actualized God's Kindness	26
Spirit Empowers God's Kindness Revealed in Jesus	51
Relational Kindness Is Healing	57
Relational Hermeneutic of Kindness: A Case Study	65
Relational Kindness and A Scientific World View	73
Relational Kindness and Courageous Action	78
Concluding Meditation	89
Summary	93
Kindness Training Exercise	97
APPENDIX A: Jesus and God Consciousness	98
APPENDIX B: Religious Poetry and Hermeneutic	103
Bibliography	127

Preface

This book is a call for kindness. Kindness is one of the first emotions known to humans, as old as mother and child. Kindness has been isolated as an evolutionary trait seen in all life forms and is a primary reason for advancement of species.

Kindness is at the core of being—

A focused awareness of being present in the here and now.

Kindness is defined as a movement

that begins in our mind and moves

to our eyes that see others as precious,

our ears that hear others with compassion,

and our hands that seek to give comfort to others.

The Kindness Blessing below is my prayer that as you read this book you will grow in kindness and help bring healing to our world.

Kindness Blessing

May kindness be in our thoughts,

making them good and loving.

May kindness be in our eyes,

leading us to see what is just in life.

May kindness be in our hands and feet

so that we may be of service to others.

May kindness be in our whole being –
Making us one with God,
one with all people,
and one with the universe.

I don't know how to define kindness,
but I know for sure when I feel it.

Kindness is the language
known around the world.

Some have objected—
Saying, kindness is simply
not in a lot of the Bible.

I would readily admit this.
War and vengeance is a big theme.

All the more reason—

We need to glean from the Bible
all the words, stories, and persons
that show kindness;

and use them as a prism
for reading the whole Bible
and all of our life experiences.

The kindness we show to ourselves, our family,
and to all living things
is the greatest healing force in the world—
Contributing to mental and physical well-being.

Introduction

"I am God, and I show mercy and kindness" (Based on Exodus 33:19, CEV).

"Our Lord, you bless those who live right, and you shield them with your kindness" (Psalm 5:11, CEV).

Jesus described his ministry in these words: "If you are tired from carrying heavy burdens, come to me and I will give you rest. . . Learn from me. I am gentle and humble, and you will find rest" (Matthew 11:28-29, CEV).

"God our Savior showed us goodness and kindness." (Titus 3:4, CEV).

"I pray that Jesus will be kind to you" (Revelation 22:21).

This book seeks to develop a relational hermeneutic of kindness for interpreting the Bible and showing its relevance for life in the world. Interpreting the Bible through the lens of kindness is especially helpful in dealing with the Bible's more difficult sections like the Judges of Israel who seem to portray a warrior God.[1] Hermeneutics is defined in the broad sense as the discipline of reflecting on how words and events of the past may become meaningful in the present.

Biblical hermeneutics begins with a grammatical analysis of the text. The first task is descriptive—finding out what the text says. Text as subject speaks to and questions the interpreter. What the text meant

---

[1] The story of Deborah as the first judge in the Old Testament is presented in a later section, pages 65-72, as a case study in hermeneutics., using kindness as the interpretive lens.

when it was first recorded does not necessarily become its meaning today. In developing a relational hermeneutic of kindness, our first task is to ask, Do the biblical writers understand God as kindness? Does the descriptive task show this? If so, then can we read all scripture through the lens of God's kindness most clearly revealed in the gentle life and tender teachings of Jesus of Nazareth? The Bible is first to be read as an historical document. Then it is interpreted through the kindness lens.

More broadly speaking, biblical hermeneutics has sought to answer two questions: What did the biblical text mean when it was written? And what does the text mean today? For many interpreters of the Bible the first question answers the second. For these interpreters, what the text meant when it was written is a timeless and eternal truth; and that is the meaning today. However, hermeneutics acknowledges a gap between the centuries that is not so easily spanned. For example, take the verse, "When God's people meet in church, the women must not be allowed to speak. They must keep quiet and listen, as the law of Moses teaches. If there is something they want to know, they can ask their husbands when they get home. It is disgraceful for women to speak in church" (1 Corinthians 14:33b-35 CEV).

The people of God have had difficulty in interpreting texts like this one that clearly reflect cultural traditions and not timeless truths. This book seeks to offer a unifying hermeneutical concept that can help us deal with difficult biblical texts like this one, and those that project human emotions of vengeance on God, feeling sure that their anger is God's anger.

The first task is to see if there is adequate support for a biblical understanding of God as one who meets each event in our lives with kindness and relates to the world in adventurous kindness. A relational hermeneutic of kindness offers an adventurous understanding of reality. Adventures are a journey into the unknown. Adventures are open-ended and can involve risk without assured results. Does the Bible understand God as non-coercive kindness, and does God meet each occasion of life with kindness?

God as Relational Kindness

This book, *A Relational Hermeneutic of Kindness*, is built on the belief that God is best understood as relational kindness. This concept of God as kindness provides the best conceptuality by which we understand the Bible, and the best route by which we find meaning in our lives and in our troubled world. A key biblical verse is— *"God, you brought me safely through birth, and you protected me as a baby at my mother's breast. From the day I was born I have been in your tender care, and from my birth you have been by my side.*[2]

Religions affirming faith in God have attempted to understand the nature of God and how God relates to the people of God and the world. In one sense God is beyond all human thoughts and wrapped in mystery. The biblical writers recognized this. Isaiah wrote that God's thoughts are not our thoughts and our ways are not God's ways.[3] Expressing his thoughts about God, Paul said, "We see in a mirror dimly" [4] and "We speak God's wisdom in a mystery."[5]

From the Bible, we know God revealed in the prophets, psalmist, and in Jesus as a uniquely personal and relational God, best described for me as creative responsive kindness. Responsive love is a phrase found often in process theology. Love is an often-used word to describe God. Jesus' gentle teachings especially capture this central truth about God in the great commandment of love. The Gospel of John and the Epistles of John make love central. I have chosen kindness as the best description of God for this reason: the word, love, has been so used and cheapened in our culture that it carries a lot of

---

[2] Author's paraphrase of Psalm 22:9-10.
[3] Isaiah 55:8-9.
[4] 1 Corinthians 13:12.
[5] 1 Corinthians 2:7.

baggage. Love focuses for most people on emotion and not action. For this reason, I have chosen to simply say, God is kind. As the creative impulse and adventurous energy that gives value to all of life, God is mystery. Yet God is present in the coming into being of all things. God calls all things into existence and tenderly guides and nurtures all things through the ages. The psalmist especially saw life in these relational terms: God, you brought me safely through birth, and you protected me as a baby at my mother's breast. From the day I was born I have been in your tender care, and from my birth you have been by my side.[6]

The Psalms are best seen as joyful songs that were grounded in the goodness of God. Psalm 5 is a good example: "Let all who run to you for protection always sing joyful songs. Provide shelter for those who truly love you and let them rejoice. Our Lord, you bless those who live right, and you shield them with your kindness."[7] Psalm 4 is an evening prayer for kindness: "There are some who ask, 'Who will be good to us?' Let your kindness, Lord, shine brightly on us. You brought me more happiness than a rich harvest of grain and grapes. I can lie down and sleep soundly because you, Lord, will keep me safe."[8]

Perhaps the greatest Psalm of loving kindness is Psalm 23. This Good Shepherd Psalm ends with these tender words: "Your kindness and love will always be with me each day of my life, and I will live forever in your house, Lord." [9] The Hebrew word, chesed, is

---

[6] Author's paraphrase of Psalm 22:9-10.
[7] Psalm 5:11-12, CEV.
[8] Psalm 4:6-8, CEV.
[9] Psalm 23:6, CEV.

found dozens of times throughout the rest of the Psalms and is often translated as loving kindness.

This image of God's kindness that Israel sang of often is also found in the Old Testament prophets like Isaiah and Hosea. Isaiah's prayer is "Please, Lord, be kind to us! We depend on you. Make us strong each morning and come to save us when we are in trouble."[10] Here is Isaiah's answer to how God heard his prayer for kindness: Our God has said, encourage my people! Give them comfort. Speak kindly to Jerusalem and announce good news: Clear a path in the desert! Make a straight road for the Lord, our God is here! Just as shepherds care for their flocks, God will carry you in arms of compassion and gently lead you.[11] Hosea speaks with the same tender image of God: When Israel was a child, I loved him, and I called my son out of Egypt. I took Israel by the arm and taught them to walk. I led them with kindness and with love, not with ropes. I held them close to me. Like a mother I bent down to feed them.[12]

In learning these sacred scriptures of his people, Jesus spiritually shook hands with Isaiah and Hosea. He daily shaped his ministry from the suffering servant songs of Isaiah and the tender story and example of Hosea. In Jesus' gentle teachings and his unique response to God's call, we see God present in the world and acting for the

---

[10] Isaiah 33:2, CEV.
[11] See Isaiah 40:1-11, CEV
[12] Hosea 11:1-4, author's paraphrase of CEV. In Hosea we especially see the tension between kindness and vengeance, a tension that runs throughout the Bible. Hosea 13 is one of the most doom filled and violent chapters in the Bible. Yet this lament chapter, like many Psalms, is preceded by the gentleness of chapter 11 and followed by chapter 14 with the promise of forgiveness and restoration, producing bountiful fruit. Jesus certainly knew both of these themes, kindness and vengeance. He chose to model kindness.

world in kind ways. In the words of Whitehead, God's "tenderness is directed toward each actual occasion, as it arises."[13]

When centered in God's creative loving kindness we live and move and have our being in a circle of kindness that takes in the whole world. God is in us and for us, in the world and for the world. In a sense, love and kindness expressed in the prophets and in Jesus do not define God; God exists before human love and kindness. God revealed in the prophets and in the gentle teachings of Jesus defines these relational terms of love and kindness for us. Jesus was responsive to God's love aims and purposes for his life and became more God conscious with each self-actualization.[14] Jesus' God consciousness, the very real existence of God in Jesus, enabled him to be more conscious of the needs of others in an ever-widening circle of loving kindness, and thus more fully divine and human. Jesus' consciousness of God is unique in that it occurred in "the fullness of time" as the culmination of more than a thousand years of covenantal history in which God nurtured Israel as a mother tenderly nurtures her child.[15]

Jesus spoke to God as a child would speak to a parent, confidently and securely. Jesus saw God like a kind father and nurturing mother.

Psalm 131 serves as a good summary of Israel's faith expressed in the prophets and modeled by Jesus, "I have learned to feel safe and

---

[13] Whitehead, op. cit., p. 105.
[14] I am using God-consciousness as Friedrich Schleiermacher did in *The Christian Faith* (2 vols.). Harper & Row, Publishers, 1963, p. 94f. I have added to Schleiermacher's use of God consciousness as a way of understanding Jesus' divinity Emmanuel Kant's "ideal of moral perfection." (See *Religion Within the Limits of Reason Alone*, pp. 54 ff.
[15] See Hosea 11 for this mother child imagery for envisioning God.

satisfied, just like a child on its mother's lap. People of God, you must trust God now and forever."[16]

God's loving kindness involves God as present in the world. Responsive love is often suffering love. God suffers with the world. We know from **personal experience** what Isaiah, Hosea, and Jesus learned: that loving kindness is a sympathetic response from one person to another. True kindness feels what the other person is feeling, rejoicing in their joys and hurting with their pains. We would doubt that a husband loves his wife if he were not aware of her feelings and if his feelings did not reflect her feelings and respond with kindness.

The biblical image of faith in the time of Jesus was of a child wrapped in the folds of a mother's garment where there is security, comfort, nurturing, love, kindness, and hope.

As we experience God revealed in the prophets, psalmist, and in Jesus, we find God rejoicing with us in our times of joy and weeping with us in our times of sorrow. Our kindness toward others is based on this responsive kindness we see in God. Our theology should reflect the awe and wonder of God being in the world, in us, and for us, holding us close as a mother wraps her child in the folds of her garments or tenderly holds her child in her lap.

The world does not exist apart from God. God the Gardener loves natural beauty. The Gardener, in tenderness, hovers over every blade of grass and whispers, "Awake. Grow. Grow beautiful and green." Meadows grow, giving way to gurgling streams, water plants, butterflies, hummingbirds, flitting from red, orange, and yellow flowers.

---

[16] Fathers also provide security, nurture, comfort, love, kindness, and hope. I am seeking a balance.

Beautiful gardens answer the call and over eons of time, all nature is lured toward ever enriching possibilities until conditions are right for life forms to emerge. Over billions of years God called forth a world able to support human beings.[17]

Humans are a new song that nature hums, the music swells with each new stanza, giving purpose and meaning. Humans moved from being gatherers in the garden to being gardeners, ever singing nature's love songs. Love, kind acts, and doing the right thing---these are all products of the garden within us that we nurture with God's guidance. Sometimes God's kindness can come through the facial expression of our grandson and granddaughter, or the touch of a friend when we are hurting. In these special moments the music becomes a joint love song that we sing to God moving us to trust God's guidance and listen to that symphony of voices within that guide us to be kind to one another.

God calls and lures the world forward in tenderness, inspiring novel love aims and goals within all parts of creation. God is supremely socially related with the purpose of sharing goodness and loving kindness with all of creation. God, all nature, and humans are interconnected. As God is immanent in the world, I am in nature and nature is in me. As I write these words, I am looking at the snow-capped Chugach Mountains of Alaska. I am in the mountains and the mountains are in me, singing their song, filling every part of my body and spirit with a wealth of beauty. Observing God's beautiful world is a centering experience of tenderness.

---

[17] God's nurturing of all things to this point gives me hope that it will all end well. See my book, *A Center that Holds: Adventures in Kindness* and the chapter on Hope for a fuller development of this theme of eschatology.

The individual as a deciding entity who sings the love songs of nature is not lost in this adventurous process of kindness for all of life is socially related. The God we meet in the beauty of nature and on the pages of the Bible, especially in the tender teachings and actions of Jesus, is in us and for us. The goodness and beauty of the natural world reflects the goodness, grace, beauty, and kindness of God. God is tenderly present in all things. This is not pantheism saying that all things are God. Rather, it is pan-en-theism, saying that God is in all things as "the poet of the world, with tender patience leading"[18] in responsive love.

The call of God toward kindness nurtured in a long covenant of love between God and Israel and supremely revealed in Jesus' tender teachings is a call to all people. In freedom some respond while others deny the call. The Bible is a record of human response to God's gentle call; it tells both the rejection and response to accept and move forward in a creative kindness with God. Some men and women responded in tender and marvelous ways in the Old Testament and New Testament times, as people have in all cultures. For Christians, Jesus is the supreme example of loving kindness. To affirm this does not lessen the role of Moses for Judaism, Mohammed for Islam or Buddha for Buddhism, and other important religious teachers. Buddha said often, "My religion is kindness." When any one relates to the God of creative possibilities, creative transformation occurs, bringing harmony and peace. **Gathering around**

---

[18] Whitehead, op. cit. p. 346.

gentle teachings that are present in most religions offers a pathway to peace in our global pluralistic age.[19]

God's loving kindness is persuasive and luring, not coercive and demanding. Relational kindness does not seek to control with coercion. Relational power is greatest in its ability to influence others. If we love someone we do not seek to control or pressure them with promises and threats. Instead we try to persuade them with tender luring love to actualize the possibilities for goodness, beauty, and kindness. The gentle Galilean glories of Jesus define power in terms of loving kindness. This is also a good theology for parenting.

Does this emphasis on God's tender persuasive power rather than coercive power make God weak? Does this question have merit? Are humans more at home with coercive power than luring and persuasive power? My parents were gentle and kind, but they were not weak. To manage a family with thirteen children required a tough tenderness, and that is how I would describe God's power.

People who want to have coercive power for themselves and for God often ask, "If God is All-powerful, why doesn't God change things?" One businessman expressed the feeling like this: "If I were God, I would show people who is boss." This man could very well have been the father of a little boy in the cartoons, down on his knees by the bedside, saying his prayers, and almost out of patience with God: "Aunt Stella isn't married yet. Uncle Hubert hasn't got a job. Daddy's hair is still falling out. I'm tired of saying prayers for this family without getting results." We all know of the silence of the sky.

---

[19] See Todd Outcalt, *The Other Jesus: Stories from World Religions* for many touch points between Judaism, Christianity, Islam, Buddhism, especially in reference to stories about the teachings and actions of Jesus. Kindness is perhaps the most important touch point.

The Book of Job turns on it. If God is Almighty as the Apostle's Creed says, why doesn't God rid the world of all its evil? The classic expression of this dilemma is this: If God is all loving, God would want to rid the world of all evil. And if God is all powerful, then God could rid the world of all evil. Since there is a very real presence of evil in the world, God must not be all loving and all powerful. As Christians we affirm that God is all loving. Thus, we need to redefine power, emphasizing not the quantity of power, but the quality of power.

The basic issue is the nature of divine power. The phrase in the Creed, "I believe in God the Father Almighty," invites us to see a different kind of power, a power qualified by a parent's love, a persuasive and luring power that sets novel aims and gently lures us toward fulfilling those aims. This parental image of God, while often overlooked, is a common view of the Bible and is seen most clearly in the gentle teachings of Jesus in the Gospels.

Is this gentle relational kindness weak? Or is gentle loving-kindness the one force that slowly but surely transforms our lives, our communities, and our world? God's kindness expressed in Trinitarian relationships and bound up in community relationships of faith, hope, love, joy, and peace may be the most powerful force in the world!

God's power expressed as a power-field of love energies issuing in kindness is transformational. These love energies are seen and experienced in God who relates to us in mysterious ways. This relational God calls all persons into this power field of love energies that transform persons and God's own self. God is first and foremost transformed by the experience of Jesus' tender life, suffering, death, and resurrection. Through Jesus' deep socially developed God-consciousness, God is revealed to us in new and transforming ways of kindness. This is God's own self-revelation. In these special relationships, God wills to be in us and for us, in the world and for the world.

In the closing chapters of *Process and Reality*, Whitehead sought to show how God relates to the world and how the world relates to God. In this major work among his philosophical writings, Whitehead was primarily concerned with elucidating the "primordial" nature of God. This aspect of God gathered all the wealth of potentiality or divine ordering of all possibilities for the world. These possibilities were further defined as God's love aims and purposes for creation. For Whitehead order was not sufficient for explaining the novelty and freshness of the new and keeping the massiveness of the order from degenerating into mere repetition. "It belongs to the goodness of the world that its settled order should deal tenderly with the faint discordant light of the dawn of another age."[20]

The satisfaction of these aims and purposes in tenderness that nothing be lost required Whitehead to present what he described as the "consequent" nature of God, i.e., God's prehension or feeling of all entities in the world. As primordial, God is unchanging in goodness, kindness, and love. As consequent, God is in the world and in us, feeling our sorrow and our joy, our hatred and our love. As we feel God's joy, love, and kindness we are changed; and as God feels our joy, love, and kindness God is changed, for this is the nature of reciprocal loving kindness. Kindness flows from the one to the many, and the many become one in the unity of the harmony of God.

---

[20] *Process and Reality*, p. 339.

My use of the metaphor, kindness as a hermeneutical term is also useful for combining both the primordial and consequent aspects of God as spelled out by Whitehead. The primordial nature of God is the ground for kindness as this quote from *Process and Reality* clearly shows: God's "tenderness is directed toward each actual occasion, as it arises."[21] Kindness does not float into the world or into our experience from nowhere. For Whitehead everything is positively somewhere in actuality and in potency everywhere. Thus, using insights from Whitehead, we can interpret kindness as the aim or goal for all of creation. And the consequent nature of God further grounds kindness as a tender care that nothing be lost. Every entity is felt by God as an actual entity. As these two roles are relational concepts, they have served as guidelines for elucidating the trinity, a doctrine that seeks to show how God relates to the people of God, first in the Scriptures and also to us. For me, kindness expresses this relationship best.

Kindness as used in the Old Testament carries well the primordial aspect of God. Kindness is a key metaphor for the way the Jewish people experienced God's aims and purposes. Exodus 33:19 defines God as kindness in this foundational "I am" saying. "I am God, and I show mercy and kindness to anyone I choose" (CEV). This verse names Kindness as an ontological aspect of God. So what the Christian belief in the Trinity names as God the Father is best conceived as "God is kind." Kindness is a gender-neutral term and communicates well what is meant by the name, Father. The faith of Israel can be stated in these three words: God is kind. The Psalms of Israel are filled with the "loving kindness" of God, and kindness is the one

---

[21] Ibid, p. 105.

unfailing response of God. The first part of the trinity can be stated as "I believe God is kind to all living things."

Kindness is also an appropriate metaphor for expressing what is intended in the second part of the Christian Trinity: The Son. Jesus responded to God's call and self-actualized in his own gentle ministry the love aims and purposes of God wrapped in kindness, becoming the model for all humanity and making it possible for God to be with us and in us in new transforming ways of kindness.

Jesus Self-Actualized God's Kindness

God's love and kindness will shine upon us like the sun that rises in the sky. On us who live in the dark shadow of death, this light will shine to guide us into a life of peace.[22]

When one tugs at a single kind word of Jesus, one finds it is attached to the heart of God.[23]

The kindness of Jesus, the bright morning star, shines throughout the New Testament, especially the Gospels of Matthew, Mark, Luke, and John. As presented in these Gospels, the kindness of Jesus reveals God's love and kindness and has transforming energy. The kindness we show to ourselves, our family, and to all living things is the greatest healing and hopeful force in the world.

The kindness of Jesus is an historical fact that is undeniable. The trend today is to deny that one can write a biography of Jesus. Albert Schweitzer's book, *The Quest of the Historical Jesus*, has been seen as the death knell to this search. My own search for the historical Jesus started in 1964 in seminary and has continued for the past fifty years. In a graduate seminar on "The Search for the Historical Jesus" we read biographies of Jesus written in English, French, and German. Since my graduate studies I have tried to keep up with the search for the historical Jesus through Rudolf Bultmann, the post-Bultmannians, and the Jesus seminars. This search has given and continues to give us valuable insight into the life and teachings of Jesus.

---

[22] Luke 1:78-79. Compare Isaiah 9:2.
[23] Dwayne Cole

My relational hermeneutic of kindness, my biblical principle of interpretation, is simply this: Jesus' kindness transforms suffering, changing our lives and our world. The abiding and eternal significance of this principle is independent of historical knowledge of Jesus, i.e., the ability to write a biography of Jesus. My writings on the gentle teachings of Jesus, for which this book dovetails nicely, demonstrate that one can write an historical account of the teachings of Jesus. The kindness of Jesus is an undeniable historical fact; and that Jesus' tender teachings and actions as the actualization of God's kindness has transforming healing power is also an historical fact well documented in personal experience.

The abiding and eternal significance of kindness as a hermeneutic for interpreting the life and teachings of Jesus is independent of historical knowledge. To use Carl Jung's thought: kindness is an archetype layered in the collective unconsciousness of most cultures. Kindness may even be isolated as an evolutionary principle. The survival of the fittest often meant being kind to insiders and creating community to offer security for growth and development. That Jesus' personal consciousness focused heavily on kindness is undeniable. Jesus self-actualized the kindness of God that he found expressed beautifully in the Psalms and prophets of his sacred Scriptures. Yet, what so

Each time we try to paint Jesus in our image he breaks free; and comes to us as one unknown, as he did to his disciples by the sea of Galilee long ago. Those who receive Jesus with fresh eyes learn in their own experience illumined by the Spirit of the risen Jesus who he is; and in following their lives are transformed by kindness.

often happens is that in writing our personal biographies of Jesus we skip over Jesus' kindness and paint Jesus from our own personal consciousness and personal interest. This is what I have learned from my fifty-year search for the historical Jesus.

I am more confident than many current biblical scholars that one can find the historical Jesus in the Gospels of the New Testament. The critical question is to what extent the kindness of Jesus is empowered by God's Spirit and united as one with God.

The miracle of the Gospels is that in and through the inspired words of the four Gospel writers, Jesus' words continue to live and speak. Gospel writing may be called an anamnesis form of writing. Anamnesis comes from the transliteration of a Greek word meaning "remembering." As acts of remembering, the gospels are not strictly speaking historical biographies about Jesus. However, this could be said for all biographical writing, for all are interpreted remembrance and not "pure" facts. There is no un-interpreted and un-biased remembering and putting remembering into written words. To be a faithful witness does not simply mean passing on tradition. The New Testament evangelists in announcing good news were responsible for letting the good news meet the changing needs of their present communities. The vital needs of the early Christian movement changed quickly and drastically following the crucifixion of Jesus.

In the anamnesis form of writing, the faithful telling of the past stories of Jesus are united with the faithful proclamation in the present worshipping communities of the evangelists. The time interval is bridged, and Spirit inspired words of Jesus are experienced. What links the past and present creating a new future is the experienced presence of God in each new act of kindness; and these are hermeneutical concerns.

The same symbiotic action can be seen in the life and teachings of Jesus. The consciousness of God's presence linked the human Jesus with Israel's prophets and psalmist, his religious past. The linking of past and present creates a new unity in Jesus' teachings, and those who hear Jesus hear the word of God. The sacred past is remembered and re-enacted in Jesus' teachings. As Jesus' mode of vision renders the past as present, when the followers of Jesus remember his tender words and actions they are linked with the historical Jesus. In remembering all are drawn into the "we circle." The core of the "we circle" are the eyewitnesses who saw and heard Jesus speak. In remembering we are linked with the "we circle" and thereby linked with the historical Jesus who becomes present to us today. Remembering overcomes the time interval. As Jesus is remembered he becomes a once for all time event. In the Church's liturgy the generations are united as one as we become one with "the great cloud of witnesses."

The act of remembering and the "we circle" formula are supported by the role of the paraclete or Spirit in the New Testament. The Spirit of God infuses and inspires the church's proclamation and the words of Jesus continue to speak, become more deeply understood, and grasped in faith. In the faithful linking of past and present, the historical Jesus steps out of the New Testament stories as they are proclaimed and into our lives as the living word of God! And this is the purpose of a relational hermeneutic.

In order to fully understand how truly kind Jesus was and see his kindness as the actualization of God's kindness, we must briefly capsule the period and environment of Jesus' life. All of life is socially related and we are shaped by the social circumstances of our life and our historical epoch. This is the meaning of the phrase in the New Testament that says, "Jesus was born in the fullness of time."[24]

The Jewish nation in Jesus' time was a small weak nation in a remote and infertile land with only a few exceptions. Since the return from the Babylonian exile, 586-538 B.C.E, the Jewish people had very little political independence. They were dominated by a long succession of foreign powers from the Persians to the Romans. Yet Israel's faith in God was like a vital nerve center that sustained her in these perilous times.

Jesus' Cultural and Social Environment

The Pharisees, seeking to sustain and strengthen faith, first appeared under the rule of John Hyrcanus (135-105 B.C.E). The name "Pharisee" is generally interpreted as "the separate ones." They had the reputation of excelling the rest of the nation in the observance of the law. This group gave birth to many of the oral laws and traditions that governed the daily life of the average Jew in Jesus' time. Jesus had to justify his gentle words and actions to the Pharisees.[25]

The Sadducees held what little political authority the Jews possessed. The Sadducean high priests were the connecting link with the foreign powers. They were a small group, more political than religious, and exercised a widespread influence. They were even harsher than the Pharisees in their dealings with Jesus.

---

[24] See Galatians 4:4.
[25] For an excellent book on the Jewish sects in the time of Jesus see Joachim Jeremias, *Jerusalem in the Time of Jesus*. This makes it all the more significant that Jesus answered God's call of kindness and conducted a ministry characterized by tenderness.

A third major Jewish sect, the Essenes, outdid the Pharisees in piety by withdrawing into small communities where they lived simple and abstentious lives. The wilderness west of the Dead Sea was a favorite location for their communities. The Dead Sea Scrolls discovered in the middle of the twentieth century have shed light on the Essenes and shown possible connections with John the Baptist and thereby Jesus. This connection is minor and could be explained by the syncretistic nature of Jewish life in the first century rather than a direct link.

The party of the Zealots made up a fourth group among the Jews. It was founded by Judas the Galilean who stirred up a rebellion against the Romans in 6 C.E.[26] The Zealots were opposed to paying tribute to pagan emperors, for God was the only true King. They usually concealed daggers and were ready to destroy the hated Romans when the opportunity was presented to them. At least one of Jesus' disciples was a Zealot.

There have been periodic attempts to tag Jesus with the "zealot" name, most recently Reza Aslan.[27] Aslan's central thesis seems to be that since Jesus grew up in Galilee where the zealot spirit was rampant, he was shaped by this spirit.[28] Aslan places a lot of weight on the one passage in Luke 22:35-38 where Jesus asked his disciples as tensions increased with the ruling authorities to sell some of their clothes and buy a sword if they did not have one. When the disciples said that they already had two swords, Jesus replied, "It is enough."

---

[26] Acts 5:37.
[27] Reza Aslan, *Zealot: The Life and Times of Jesus of Nazareth*.
[28] No doubt this is partly true. A thesis of this chapter is that one is shaped by one's epoch and this partly accounts for the diversity of the Bible written over a thousand year period. However there are individuals who are able to rise above the spirit of their times, and Jesus was one of these persons.

This could be translated, "It is enough about that!" It was common advice to take a sword on dangerous trips in the time of Jesus. This advice is found only in Luke 22:37; and Luke places it in the context of a quote from Isaiah 53:12, a suffering servant song. The spirit of the suffering servant who willingly gives life would certainly give a new slant to this advice of buying a sword.

Jesus' response after the remark about already having two swords would seem to support this interpretation. In frustration about the disciples not understanding his role, Jesus says, in effect, "that is enough about swords." The one clear principle from Jesus' life and teachings is that one has the right to give life but never to take life.[29] History shows many examples of men and women who rose above the spirit of their times and became shapers of events not followers –Abraham Lincoln, Ghandi, Martin Luther King, Jr., and Mother Teresa to name a few.

The Herodians are mentioned in the New Testament as enemies of Jesus, both in Galilee[30] and in Jerusalem.[31] The term apparently denotes an attitude rather than a political party or religious sect. It seems to refer to the Jews who supported the Herodian rule and the Romans.

The vast majority of Palestinian Jews were unaffiliated with any of these groups. These multitudes were known as people of the land,

---

[29] To be sure Jesus struggled with all of these human responses to God and to others. His own disciples according to John 6 tried to force him to become their king. Jesus' temptations can be seen as a time when Jesus struggled with the nature of his life and teachings. What kind of leader and teacher would he be? Jesus came down on the side of a suffering servant like Second Isaiah and the gentle example of Hosea.
[30] Mark 3:6.
[31] Matthew 22:16; Mark 12:13.

"Am-haaretz." The Pharisees felt that these common people from the country were ignorant of or indifferent to the Mosaic law; thus, they were considered immoral and irreligious.

Without excluding the others, it was more self-exclusion, it was basically this group of common people who were recipients of Jesus' gentle, Galilean teachings. Though the Pharisees saw them as worthless outcasts, Jesus saw them with compassion because they were helpless like "sheep without a shepherd."[32] Jesus chose to become like the Good Shepherd of Psalm 23 and Ezekiel 34, tenderly caring for the poor and needy. In choosing this path, Jesus perfectly incarnated the kindness of God expressed in Israel's best faith and practice. In choosing kindness, Jesus consciously rejected the path of the zealots, the path of vengeance.

Jesus' Birth and Early Years

The simplicity and gentleness of the birth narratives of Jesus and his tender teachings are all the more striking against the Jewish cultural and social background given above. The nativity scene evokes the best feelings in our human nature: the devout mother and father, the child in a bare manger, the shepherds and wise men who come to worship him, and the angels who bridge the lowly earthly scene with the heavenly spheres, a bridging which the life, death, and resurrection of Jesus would make complete.

It is almost unbelievable! The human Jesus was born in a remote nation in the humblest of circumstances and was cradled in a manger, perhaps a feed trough.[33] Yet, in these humble circumstances, the

---

[32] Matthew 9:36.
[33] It is important to see that the birth of Jesus did not violate our understanding of human nature.

baby Jesus was surrounded by gentle Mary and Joseph, simple shepherds, and glorious angelic choruses. The Gospel writers, writing 70-90 years after the birth of Jesus, were able to see from the gentle teachings of Jesus how God and Jesus had become one in kindness; and see how Jesus' faithful response to God's call enabled God to come near to people. In Luke's words, God came in tenderness and the bright light of heaven shone upon all who walked in darkness.[34] Whitehead interpreted this as God meeting each rising occasion with tenderness. Jesus responded to the call of God and revealed God's kindness in his tender teachings.

Luke's Gospel is the only one which has anything to say about Jesus' early years. After the shepherds' visit, the story continues with the circumcision of the child on the eighth day of his life; in fulfillment of the law the child was formally given the Greek name Jesus which is the same as Joshua in Hebrew.[35] It was a common name meaning "he saves" or in its full form, "Jehovah saves." The presentation of Jesus in the Temple places us once again in the very heart of Jewish piety and worship. In keeping with the Mosaic law, Mary observed the purification rites by presenting an offering of a pair of doves or two young pigeons while at the same time presenting the child to God.[36] The offering indicates that Mary and Joseph were poor. According to Leviticus 12, the offering called for a lamb but mothers who were poor could substitute the less expensive offering.

In the Temple, Joseph and Mary encountered a good, God-fearing man named Simeon who was waiting for Israel to be saved. When Simeon took Jesus in his arms to bless him--an appropriate symbol

---

[34] Luke 1:78.
[35] Luke 2:21; cf. Genesis 17:9-14; Leviticus 12:3.
[36] Leviticus 12:1-4, 6; Luke 2:22-24.

for the one who would later take children in his arms and bless them--Simeon burst forth in praise to God: Now Lord, you have kept your promise, and you may let your servant go in peace. With my own eyes I have seen your salvation, which you have prepared in the presence of all peoples: a light to reveal your will to the Gentiles and bring glory to your people Israel.[37]

There was also in the Temple an elderly prophetess, a widow named Anna (Hannah in Hebrew). Anna worshipped God day and night, fasting and praying, never leaving the Temple. She too recognized who the baby was and with thanksgiving to God "spoke about the child to all who were waiting for God to set Jerusalem free."[38]

Having completed the requirements of the law, Joseph, Mary, and Jesus returned to their home town of Nazareth in Galilee. In Galilee Jesus grew and became strong, increasing in favor (graciousness) with God and with humans.[39]

These birth and infancy narratives are stamped throughout with the mark of Jewish piety. We meet Judaism at its best as the cradle of Jesus. We see humble, lowly, gentle servants of God who have spent their whole lifetime glorifying God and waiting patiently for God's deliverance and salvation.

These accounts make it clear that God comes to waiting people, taking the initiative and drawing near to them. In kindness God came to lift up the lowly and gentle servants.[40] The heart throb of tenderness and gentleness beats throughout. Not only is God kind and

---

[37] Luke 2:29-32.
[38] Luke 2:36-38.
[39] Luke 2:52.
[40] Titus 3:4; Luke 1:48, 52.

gentle, Joseph is gentle and considerate of Mary. Joseph was a bridge for Jesus' understanding of one who would become a heavenly Father to him.

Also, we have seen that the lowly are exalted or glorified. Heavenly glories shine throughout these narratives and will continue to shine through Jesus' gentle Galilean glories. When reading these Gospel accounts of the birth of Jesus we need to remember that they were written 70-90 years after the birth of Jesus, and while they are historical, they have naturally taken on some legendary and mythic qualities.

The only other glimpse of Jesus the Gospels gives us of his early years was his visit to the Temple at the age of twelve. On this visit Mary and Joseph miss Jesus and began to look for him. They find him in the Temple asking serious questions and saying, I must be about My Father's business.[41]

This seems to be a very significant time in Jesus' maturation. The kindness, gentleness, and love of God that had been prefigured in Mary and Joseph and his faith community were now affirmed as being rooted in God. While this was a significant insight or rite of passage for Jesus, he went back to Galilee with Joseph and Mary where he continued to grow in body and in wisdom, gaining favor with God and humans. The Greek word translated as "favor" here is a form of χαρις. It is usually translated in the New Testament as grace. It can also be translated as kindness.[42] It describes the

---

[41] Luke 2:49. While these stories have taken on legendary tones they still reflect historical events.
[42] The American Bible Society's *Contemporary English Version* often translates χαρις as kindness. See below for a treatment of χαρις. I have checked the usage of this

qualities of grace and kindness that make a person attractive or favorable. It also describes the attitude of goodwill, respect, or approval of others toward a gracious and kind person.

Jesus returned home to Galilee. Home for Jesus included four brothers: James, Joseph, Judas, and Simon. He also had sisters, but we are not told how many nor are we told their names. Clearly Jesus grew up in a large household which was no doubt lively. Having grown up in a family where I was the eighth of thirteen children, I can vouch for this.

How much formal education Jesus received is not known. Joseph would have started Jesus' education in the home as the Jewish law commanded. Every pious Jewish father, and we are told that Joseph was devout,[43] taught his son the Shema: Israel, remember this! The Lord--and the Lord alone--is our God. Love the Lord your God with all your heart, with all your soul, and with all your strength. Never forget these commandments that I am giving you today, i.e., center your life on these teachings of love. Teach them to your children.[44] Jesus made this the first commandment of all of his teachings.[45] It is interesting that Jesus added "with all your mind" to his presentation of the great commandment. We know that Jesus had an active and perceptive mind.

In addition to learning from Joseph at home, Jesus probably attended the synagogue school in Nazareth. How much, if any, formal

---

word from Plato up through the time of Jesus and found that they are justified in translating χαρις as kindness. See my *Book of Revelation: Jesus' Kindness Transforms Suffering*, where I used kindness as my hermeneutic for interpreting John's message to the suffering followers of Jesus in the seven Churches.
[43] Matthew 1:19.
[44] Deuteronomy 6:4-7.
[45] Mark 12:28-30.

education he had, of course, is not known. A popular view today is to see Jesus as a simple uneducated carpenter. The Gospels themselves point in the other direction. In the Gospel of Mark, the verb, "teach" occurs seventeen times, and in all but one of these Jesus is the subject. Jesus is very often called teacher by his disciples and his opponents. The fact that Jesus was called teacher by his opponents would seem to indicate that they recognized his qualification to teach. According to Luke, Jesus read the Scripture lesson in the synagogue at Nazareth.[46] In his teaching he assumed that his hearers had heard their scriptures read and some probably had read some biblical scrolls. He would often ask, "Have you not read...?[47] Jesus had an almost encyclopedic knowledge of his Holy Scriptures and with penetration and independence he combined and interpreted them in a unique way. Jesus read and spoke Aramaic. He knew Hebrew well enough to read it in the synagogue. He, of economic necessity, had a carpenter's command of common Greek, which was becoming the common language of his day. Jesus' study of the Old Testament Scriptures helped to shape his understanding of his ministry and message. This was especially true of the Suffering Servant passages of Isaiah.

Kindness in Jesus' Teachings

God's love and kindness will shine upon us like the sun that rises in the sky. On us who live in the dark shadow of death, this light will shine to guide us into a life of peace (Luke 1:78-79, CEV).

---

[46] Luke 4:16-20.
[47] Mark 2:25, 12:10; Matthew 12:5; 19:4; 21:16, 42.

The goal of the Christian should be to live in harmony with the kind teachings of Jesus.

> Simple acts of kindness to oneself, one's family, and to all living things are the most powerful transformers in the world.

Serving for almost fifty years as a parish minister, I learned a lot about the need for tenderness in our human relationships. We all fight hard battles and need at least a bushel of kindness a day. Every person and every family needs gentleness to survive.

My own father and mother were examples of kindness for me and my six brothers and six sisters. My father often prayed public prayers in our little country Church, and one of his favorite expressions was "Kind Father." He started his prayers with this address and repeated it several times throughout the prayer. He said it so many times that I was embarrassed about it. Of course, it doesn't take much to embarrass an adolescent when it comes to his or her parents.

Today I treasure this memory and it has helped me to be a kinder person. My mother and father taught me by word and example that God is kind. They were gentle and loving parents and they made it easy for all thirteen of us to believe in a gentle and loving God. For their children, parents truly are the first bridge to the love of God, as are all caregivers.

This book springs from this source and holds up the kindness of Jesus as the guiding light for our lives, our Churches, and our world. It is the nature of light to draw us in to its center and reveal newness. The Gospel of Luke expresses this truth well: *God's love and kindness will shine upon us like the sun that rises in the sky. On us who live in the dark shadow of death, this light will shine to guide us into a life of peace.*[48]

In contrast to the bleak gray of much of Palestine, Galilee, especially the plain of Gennesaret, was a very fertile, magnificent garden, inspiring Jesus' bio-philic (love of life) teachings. Jesus preached gentle Galilean glories in this delightful countryside. The flowers of the fields, birds of the air, farmers sowing seed, and fishermen casting their nets all came into Jesus' teachings and parables. This earthly beauty gave Jesus a vision of heavenly glory; and the vision was grounded in earthly realities, shining on the highways and byways of Galilee in Jesus' tenderness and gentleness, transforming lives.

Let me hasten to say that Galilee was not all sweetness and light, neither was the rugged carpenter from Nazareth. Not for a minute do I imply that with this theme of kindness. Personally speaking, I had to learn to balance kindness and toughness in my own life. I grew up as the eighth of thirteen children on a working farm and life was sometimes rough as a cob. I played football for four years of high school, playing both offensive and defensive right end for the whole game. I worked in a wire mill on the "graveyard" shift to help pay my way through college. In that mill I received a real lesson about toughness and heard plenty of "gutter" language that was more suitable for the halls of hell than the halos of heaven. At least this experience prepared me for unruly deacon and elder meetings in the church more than seminary did. Building houses for seven years and going through great success and failure also revealed a tough side of life to me. However, my basic nature still tilts toward

---

[48] Luke 1:78-79, CEV.

tenderness due to my family background and the gentle teachings of Jesus seem to reveal the same about Jesus. As Jesus worked through his own temptations and chose kindness as his guiding principle for interpreting the scriptures and life situations, each of us has to choose our way. I have chosen kindness as my way.

This background makes Jesus' kindness all the more amazing with transforming centering power. Jesus' disciples were slowly transformed by Jesus' gentle teachings and actions. And the kindness of Jesus is a vision of world peace for every age.

Jesus' Gentle and Kind Words

Does the New Testament verify that Jesus was gentle and kind? The Greek New Testament does not have just one term for kindness. Several Greek words are used by different writers to describe gentleness in its various aspects. The same is true of other concepts like love (αγαπη, ερος, φιλια). The Greek terms that best denote the gentle attitude are πραυς and πραυτης.

Πραυς, Πραυτης (gentle, gentleness)

In reference to persons, πραυς and πραυτης, the noun and adjective form, are best translated as gentle and gentleness. The two terms are used about 15 times in the Greek New Testament and may also be translated as kind, meek, humble, friendly, or pleasant, in both adjective and noun forms. As used in these different forms the words imply gentleness as opposed to rough, harsh, or violent. Gentleness is a synonym of ελεος, mercy. It is an active attitude not passive submission.

Among the Greeks, a kind, gentle, and friendly attitude toward family and friends was highly prized. It was the quality of a great soul like Socrates. However, it was alright to be harsh to one's enemies. For Plato πραυς was the mark of the ideal kingdom. For Aristotle it was a mean between anger which had a positive value and indifference.

In its Hebrew form, πραυς is used twelve times in the Old Testament. It is used only once in the Pentateuch, the first five books of the Old Testament, but it is a significant summary description of the great leader, Moses---"Moses was a humble (gentle) man, more humble than anyone else on earth."[49]

In the Old Testament kindness is rooted in God. The inheritance of the land promised to Abraham and his descendants comes to the gentle who wait— "The humble will possess the land and enjoy prosperity and peace."[50]

These eschatological overtones are expressed as a messianic prophecy in Zechariah 9:9, "Rejoice, rejoice, people of Zion! Shout for joy, you people of Jerusalem! Look, your king is coming to you! He comes triumphant and victorious, but gentle and riding on a donkey."

In the New Testament, the mission of Jesus is the fulfillment of gentleness. In fact, it is the self-designation of Jesus in Matthew 11:28-30--"Come to me, all of you who are tired from carrying heavy loads, and I will give you rest. Take my yoke and put it on you, and learn from me, because I am gentle and humble in spirit; and you will find

---

[49] Numbers 12:3.
[50] Psalm 37:9-11.

rest. For the yoke I will give you is easy and the load I will put on you is light." In interpreting the New Testament, the titles and descriptions that Jesus applies to himself should carry the greatest weight. Jesus did not hesitate to say, "I am gentle."

In fulfillment of eschatological hope, Jesus said, "Blessed are the gentle, they will receive what God has promised!"[51] As a further fulfillment of prophecy,[52] Jesus entered Jerusalem on what we call Palm Sunday as king---"Now this occurred to fulfill what was spoken by the prophet: 'Tell the daughter of Zion your King is now coming to you, Gentle, and riding on a donkey, Yea, on the colt of a beast of burden.'"[53]

This self-designation of Jesus as gentle is all the more significant when set against the zealot and political messianic expectations of the first century in Galilee. The Gospel of John tells us that after the feeding of the five thousand these feelings were so strong that the crowd came and sought to force Jesus to become their king.[54]

That Jesus was πραυς, tender of heart, is also supported by the Letters of Paul in the New Testament and in non-biblical sources like the Gospel of Thomas, the Sibylline Oracles, and Pistis Sophia. In Second Corinthians chapter ten, verse one, Paul wrote, "Jesus himself was humble and gentle." Colossians 3:12 grounds kindness in the being of God, "You are God's people so be gentle, kind, humble, and meek." Titus 3:4 also describes God as kind.

---

[51] Matthew 5:5.
[52] Zechariah 9:9, quoted above.
[53] Matthew 21:4-5. Williams translation.
[54] John 6:14-15.

ταπεινος, ταπεινοω, ταπεινωσις

This group of Greek words occurs thirty-four times in the New Testament, and they are usually translated "lowly", but they carry the connotation of kindness and gentleness. Here we will be concerned for the one occurrence that refers to Jesus. Again, it is significant in that it is a self- designation, like πραυς. Jesus said of himself, "I am gentle (πραυς) and lowly (ταπεινοω) of heart (Matthew 11:29).

χρηστος

Jesus used χρηστος twice, once to describe the nature of God as kind to the ungrateful and wicked[55] and once as a self-designation, describing himself as one who is kind or merciful in what he requires of those who come to him.[56] It is important to see how χρηστος was used in the Septuagint in reference to God. A key passage is found in Exodus 34:6, "I am who I am, and I am kind and patient with my people, I show great love and I can be trusted." Here kindness takes on the quality of good character. God can be trusted to act with loving kindness toward the people of God, and this is the basis of the covenant God forms with the people of God. Even when Israel failed God, God continued to be kind and forgiving. In this context kindness takes on the qualities of patience and forgiveness.

Paul understood kindness in this way as well. In Romans 2:4 he writes about the "fullness of the χρηστητος, kindness, of God and God's patience, μακροθυμιας. In Romans 11:22 Paul speaks of the kindness of God being shown for the ones who have fallen away from God. In these uses of kindness Paul is true to the Old

---

[55] Luke 6:35.
[56] Matthew 11:30.

Testament understanding of the gracious action of God and he sees this fulfilled in the actions of Jesus. In Galatians 5:22-23 Paul listed kindness as one of the fruits of the Spirit that should be growing in the life of Christians.

1 Peter 2:2-3, shows the saving action of kindness. "Like new born infants, long for the pure spiritual milk, so that by it you may grow into salvation. If indeed you have tasted that the Lord is good and kind, χρηστος.

The crowning verse on kindness in the New Testament for Christians is Ephesians 4:32---"Be kind and merciful, and forgive others, just as God forgave you because of Christ." This key verse links kindness with forgiveness and anchors these qualities in God's own actions with the gentle ministry of Jesus.

ελεος

Ελεος occurs three times in Matthew and is usually translated as mercy. The Good News Bible translates it as kindness, its original Old Testament meaning. This can be seen in Matthew 9:9-11, which reports Jesus' call of Matthew to discipleship. After Jesus called Matthew, he was having a meal in Matthew's house with other tax collectors and outcasts. Some Pharisees saw this and asked Jesus' disciples, "Why does Jesus eat with such people?" Jesus heard them and answered, "People who are well do not need a doctor, but only those who are sick. Go and find out what is meant by the scripture that says, 'It is kindness that I want, not animal sacrifices.' I have not come to call respectable people, but outcasts." This and the other two passages in Matthew 12:7; 23:23 characterize Jesus' ministry as merciful kindness toward the outcasts and demand the same for the disciples who would follow Jesus.

Ελεος, mercy, occurs six times in Luke. Five of these are in the birth announcements of John and Jesus and refer to the wonderful kindness and tender mercy God is showing toward the people of God.[57] Luke 1:78 is most relevant to the theme of "Gentle Galilean Glories:" "Our God is merciful and tender. God will cause the bright dawn of salvation to rise on us and to shine from heaven on all those who live in the dark shadow of death, to guide our path to peace."

σπλαγχνον, σπλανγχνιζομαι

In Luke 1:78, ελεος is combined with σπλαγχνον and is translated as "tender mercy." The verb form, σπλαγχνιζομαι, occurs twelve times in Matthew, Mark, and Luke, the Synoptic Gospels, and is usually translated as "having compassion." Ten of these represent Jesus as one in whom divine compassion is present. Jesus is moved with compassion toward a man with a dreaded skin disease,[58] the crowd of people who were like sheep without a shepherd,[59] and the hungry crowd.[60]

Jesus also had compassion on the widow of Nain and raised her dead son back to life[61], and with compassion he restored sight to two blind men.[62] The verb, having compassion, also had a central place in three of Jesus' most significant parables: the unforgiving servant who had been forgiven with compassion,[63] the good Samaritan whose heart was filled with compassion when he saw the wounded man

---

[57] Luke 1:50, 54, 58, 72, 78.
[58] Mark 1:41.
[59] Mark 6:34; Matthew 14:14.
[60] Mark 8:2; Matthew 15:32.
[61] Luke 7:11-17.
[62] Matthew 20:29-34.
[63] Matthew 18:21-35, See verse 34.

lying by the roadside,[64] and the parable of the prodigal son, better called the waiting father, for it is the father who saw the son a long way off and had compassion and ran to meet him.[65]

In all of these teachings of Jesus that use σπλαγχνον and σπλαγχνιζομαι, Jesus' human emotions are described in the strongest terms possible in order to stress the tender compassion with which God claims persons in saving grace. This was also true of all the other Greek words we have studied.

χαρις

The χαρις word group appears about 175 times in the New Testament, with the majority occurring in the Epistles of Paul. Most English versions of the Bible translate χαρις as grace or gracious. However, the *Contemporary English Version* of the American Bible Society almost always translates χαρις as kindness. A survey of the history of the term from its early Greek origins to the time of the New Testament justifies this use of kindness. In both the Old Testament and the New Testament, the Hebrew and Greek words usually translated as grace imply a kind turning of one person to another in an act of assistance. God's covenant grace also implies kindness.

Perhaps the most significant uses of χαρις come in the Book of Revelation. At a time when the followers of Jesus are being persecuted and dying for their faith, John the writer of Revelation holds up a vision of the kind Jesus. The book starts with this prayer: "I pray that you will be blessed with kindness and peace from God, who is

---

[64] Luke 10:25-37, see v. 33. The whole act of the Samaritan was summarized as an act of kindness, see v. 37.
[65] Luke 15:11-32, see v. 20.

and was and is coming. May you receive kindness and peace from Jesus, the faithful witness."[66] Revelation ends with this prayer: "I pray that Jesus will come soon and be kind to all of you."[67]

Yes, Jesus was gentle, lowly, and kind. The word clusters we have examined leave no room for doubt. What struck me was how Jesus described himself as being gentle. Thus, we are on solid ground when we speak of Jesus as kindness. The kindness of God shines in the words and deeds of Jesus. The disciples and the crowds who followed Jesus saw the glory of God shining through his gentle Galilean glories. Can there be any doubt that Jesus lived and taught kindness? The rich cluster of words described above make kindness a good choice for our relational hermeneutic of kindness.

Importance of Kindness Today

It is my conviction that kindness rings true in most cultures and can be a unifying and centering theme for dialogue in this global pluralistic age between most religions of the world, offering a path to peace. Following the amazing discoveries of the genome project, the mapping of the human chromosomes, biologists speak of the genetic unity of all living things, believing that all organisms descended from the same ancestral life forms. Thus far the genome project has shown that the common ancestor of all living things was similar to single-celled microbes with the simplest molecular composition that goes back several billion years. Thus all life shares a molecular history and is interrelated, interconnected.

---

[66] Based on Revelation 1:4-5 from the Greek New Testament.
[67] Based on Revelation 22:20-21, from the Greek New Testament. For a fuller treatment of this use of χαρις as kindness in Revelation see my book, *The Book of Revelation: Jesus' Kindness Transforms Suffering*.

This unifying dialogue must take place if we are to have reconciliation between the world religions and find a route to peace. The greatest challenge to theistic religions is the pervasive reality of evil and the misery it leaves in its wake. This unifying and centering theme of kindness is one possible solution to this problem, especially the growing divide between Christianity and Islam.

"Loving kindness" is a major theme in Judaism. The Psalms of the Old Testament are full of this concept that is key to understanding God and God's people. Since Judaism gave birth to Christianity and Islam, the two largest religions in the world, this unifying theme is something all three religions hold in common. "Metta" is a strong concept in Buddhism and carries the meaning of loving kindness or unconditional love. Buddha often spoke of loving kindness as everything. Loving kindness is taught without attachment. In much Buddhist thought love when practiced moves from self to friend, to enemy, and to all beings everywhere. "Karuna" or compassion that leads one to assist others is also key. Meaningful dialogue could be held around the theme of gentle teachings that could transform the relationships between these major religions.

Also, the longer I have lived with the New Testament the more I have become convinced that a major thrust of these sacred scriptures is to show the humanity of Jesus. This makes Jesus' sacrificial death on the cross more meaningful with more transforming power. This approach also opens the door to see that other major religious leaders like Moses, Confucius, Mohammed, Buddha, Gandhi, and Martin Luther King, Jr. can also self-actualize creative love aims and purposes that transform lives and our world.

One may not be able to write a biographical account of the life of Jesus. As seen above, I do believe you can locate in the Gospels the authentic teachings of Jesus, like the gentle teachings. Whether they all come from Jesus or some of them are born as a product of the Gospel writers or the early church community, really do not matter in one sense. They are inspired by Jesus' gentle ministry and remain insightful, challenging teachings than can change and transform lives and offer a path to peace.

Jesus' Galilean vision of kindness has flickered through many cultures since the time of Jesus, but it has never been fully realized. Yet it still holds the promise of creative advance, a center that holds, and world transformation.

Spirit Empowers God's Kindness Revealed in Jesus

God as relational kindness lured creation out of chaos. God as Gentle Spirit filled the lives of the prophets who spoke God's message. God's Spirit was present in the birth of Jesus. The same Spirit descended upon Jesus at his baptism and energized Jesus' gentle ministry. Spirit empowered Jesus' followers in Pentecost activity to continue his tender words and actions after the crucifixion and resurrection of Jesus.

The basic role of Spirit in the New Testament is to be an encourager. By linking Spirit with the continuing ministry of Jesus, the New Testament writers join kindness and encouragement. The Hebrew word for Spirit is ruach; and this Hebrew word can be translated as wind or breath of life. It is the word used in Genesis for God breathing the breath of life into humans. This is the way John in Revelation used Spirit in referring to the two witnesses who proclaimed God's message and became martyrs: "Spirit of life is breathed into them by God" (Revelation 11:11). This use of Spirit as the breath of life would have special significance for Jesus' followers in John's churches who are dying as martyrs.

John in Revelation, as does most of the New Testament, virtually equates Spirit and the risen Jesus, seeing their role as one as in Revelation 19:10, "Everyone who tells about Jesus does it by the power of Spirit." For John the church is the new body in which the risen Jesus lives, meeting each rising occasion with the spirit of kindness.

The risen Jesus walks in the churches, sees their strengths and weaknesses, and offers to them the centering path to transformation.[68]

In the churches in Ephesus, Smyrna, Pergamum, Thyatira, Sardis, Philadelphia, and Laodicea the Risen Jesus lives and continues his gentle teachings that bring kindness and peace. Revelation 1:5 is addressed to all the churches and captures this consoling truth: "May kindness and peace be yours from Jesus Christ, the faithful witness" (CEV). The role of Jesus and the role of Spirit are one in this compassionate transforming work.

In the prologue to the Gospel of John, God as creative life-giving Word is seen as coming into the world in human form in Jesus to bring heavenly light into a dark world. It is important to see that in the prologue as a whole Jesus as a human person cannot be separated from the divine presence of God. John accomplishes this by presenting Jesus as the incarnation of the logos (word). This linkage allows us to see how the human Jesus is different from God but at the same time one with God as a single entity in creating and redeeming.

While John does not connect logos (word) and Sophia (wisdom) with the gift of Spirit in the prologue he does equate risen Jesus and Spirit later in his Gospel as we will see below. Luke and Paul make the connection between Jesus, wisdom, and Sprit in their writings. Luke says that as Jesus matured, he was filled with σοφια (wisdom) and χαρις (kindness, grace).[69] Sophia as the feminine companion of God at creation played an important role in Jewish wisdom literature

---

[68] The Book of Revelation, while it is not often recognized, has more teaching on the trinity than any other book of the Bible. See my development of the theme of kindness as a trinitarian metaphor in *The Book of Revelation: Jesus' Kindness Transforms Suffering*.
[69] Luke 2:40, 52.

as can be seen in Proverbs 8. Luke in Acts 6:3 connects σοφιας (wisdom) and πνευματος (spirit) as the traits of a good leader.

In 1 Corinthians 12:7-8, Paul connects spirit and wisdom: "The Spirit has given each of us a special way of serving others. Some of us can speak with wisdom while others can speak with knowledge, but these gifts come from the same Spirit." For Paul the continuing ministry of Jesus is empowered by God's Spirit: "You are no longer ruled by the desires of the flesh, but by God's Spirit, who dwells in you. People who don't have the Spirit of the Risen Jesus in them don't belong to Jesus."[70]

In the Gospel of John this union of Jesus and Spirit is affirmed. In the upper room discourse John reports Jesus as saying, "I won't leave you like orphans. I will come back to you. In a little while the people of the world won't be able to see me, but you will see me. And because I live, you will live."[71] Here Spirit and risen Jesus are one; Jesus is Spirit. Spirit is given to continue the kind teachings of Jesus about forgiveness: "Then Jesus breathed on them and said, 'Receive the Spirit. If you forgive anyone's sins, they will be forgiven."[72]

The Gospel of John has four occurrences of παρακλητος (paraclete) and 1 John has one. This Greek word is formed by joining παρα (by the side of) and κλητος (called) and is best translated as one who is "called to walk along the side of" Jesus' followers in all ages to offer encouragement by meeting each rising occasion with tenderness.

---

[70] My translation of Romans 8:9.
[71] John 14:18-19.
[72] John 20:22-23.

The Epistle of James equates Spirit and σοφια (wisdom) in 1:5 and 3:17 as does Ephesians 1:17. In each case the feminine form of σοφια carries the connotations of kindness. Ephesians opens with the common epistolary greeting: "I pray that God our Father and our Lord Jesus Christ will be kind to you and will bless you with peace."[73] This prayer for kindness is followed by spiritual blessings seen in Jesus' sacrifice on the cross.[74] Then comes another prayer: "I ask the glorious Father and God of our Lord Jesus Christ to give you his Spirit. The Spirit will make you wise (Sophia) and let you understand what it means to know God."[75] The message of these verses is that God is kind, Jesus is kind, and Spirit is kind.

In 1 John 2:1, paraclete is linked with Jesus. In the verses that follow 2:1, the role of Spirit is to enable the followers of Jesus to obey his commandments of love and kindness. Clearly the role of Spirit is to continue the kindness of God's presence in the tender teachings of Jesus.

The Epistle of 1 Peter linked God and Spirit with kindness and with Jesus' suffering on the cross. This Epistle actually used the name, Christ, instead of Jesus, but by linking it with the historical suffering of the cross we are justified in saying that Spirit is equated with kindness and with Jesus. We can see this linkage most clearly in the CEV: "Some prophets told how kind God would be to you, and they searched hard to find out more about the way you would be saved.

---

[73] Ephesians 1:2. CEV.
[74] Ephesians 1:3-14.
[75] Ephesians 1:17. CEV.

The Spirit of Christ (Jesus) was in them and was telling them how Christ (Jesus) would suffer and then would be given great honor."[76]

All the New Testament writers explored above could write of the risen Jesus and Spirit in the same sentence and make them interchangeable.[77] When discussing God, Jesus, and Spirit we are talking about mystery filled relationships. Let me try to make it as clear as possible. The name, Spirit, is best equated with God's presence in the risen Jesus. The role of Spirit/Risen Jesus is to continue the gentle, kind, love teachings of the historical Jesus in his new body, the church.

Thus, in summary we can say there is adequate biblical support, using the simplest of terms, to say, God is kind, Jesus is kind, and Spirit is kind. One test of an adequate biblical hermeneutic is whether it can unify the diverse biblical themes and give meaning to our lives.

John's vision of heaven in Revelation

lifts everything from earth to heaven,

starting with the crucified Jesus,

the Lamb that was slain.

The suffering of Jesus

is brought before the throne of God

and absorbed in creative responsive love.

In this divine action

union with God as One is completed

---

[76] 1 Peter 1:10-11.
[77] Romans 8:9-11.

and transformed into heavenly reality
as the risen Jesus passes back into the world
as a new creation.
The risen Jesus gathers a community,
as a mother hen gathers her chicks.
In this community the risen Jesus lives
and continues his ministry
empowered by God's Spirit,
the same Spirit that empowered the prophets,
Jesus' historical ministry,
and spiritual leaders in other faith traditions.
The hermeneutic of kindness is about this Spirit of inclusion
that joins all love energies into one redemptive healing force
that has the power to change our lives and our world.

Relational Kindness Is Healing

A relational hermeneutic of kindness seeks to understand God and how God relates to all creation with noncoercive kindness. This is in contrast to much traditional theology that is based on a mechanistic model that sees the world as made up of unchanging building blocks that bounce like billiard balls when hit by the cue stick. Protons and atoms bounce off each other unaffected in this static view, giving a view of cosmic and biological evolution as re-arrangement of the building blocks.

Using kindness as a relational hermeneutic says that in the course of evolution change occurs in subjects, not objects. In traditional theology based on understanding the universe as a mechanistic universe of unchanging objects, God manipulates and causes all things that happen; even accidents and natural disasters are interpreted from this perspective. The Bible portrays the shadow side of human nature and since this human earthly nature is always connected on another level to the divine heavenly nature, we should not try to separate the two levels in the Bible. Kindness unifies these experiences and brings healing from personal tragedy. I witnessed this healing many times in my ministry. In meeting each occasion of our life experiences with kindness, God's novel love aims and purposes are shaped in our lives through persuasion, not coercion.

I grew up with this traditional view of God's coercive action—that God causes all things, even cruel accidents. As a senior in high school I began to question this unworthy view of God.

Wendell was my best friend from the time we entered the first grade in school. We did all the things boys typically did growing up in the rural South in the post- depression decades of the forties and fifties.

On the school grounds we played marbles and the daring game of follow the leader, which took us on adventures through the surrounding woods. In high school we played baseball and football. Wendell was a big guard in football, and he was good enough to consider a college and pro career. I was a lean and mean right end playing on both the offensive and defensive teams and lucky to be injury free after four years of tackling and being tackled. After canning his opposing guard, Wendell would make sure my lane stayed open on short pass plays. In fact, he could be one of the reasons I survived largely unscathed.

Then it happened. Just two weeks before graduation, Wendell was killed when two cars collided head-on at a curve in the road. His older brother, who was driving drunk, was injured but fully recovered, at least physically. The two elderly people in the other car, who were outstanding citizens and active church members were both also killed instantly. When I learned of the accident, I was stunned and filled with grief.

I remember going home from the funeral and climbing on the old Allis Chalmers farm tractor to cultivate the fields. I wanted to be alone with my troubling thoughts undisturbed. Soon a thunderstorm began to form and the sky darkened, as though nature was in sympathy with my dark mood.

>Lightning flashed and thunder rolled. I cried out in the spirit
>>of Job, shaking my fist at the heavens,
>>>Why, O God,
>>>>did Wendell
>>>>>die

in this terrible car collision?

Why do you

make and then

break

such a strong

youth?

Did you really need another flower

in heaven, as the preacher said?

No answer came. The clouds were not rolled back, and there was no voice from heaven. But the storm passed on. The gentle rain came and washed away my tears. As the tractor rumbled on, I had a deep feeling of God's presence. A sparkling rainbow appeared on the horizon, and I found strength and hope in the glow of the rainbow to go on with my life.

Feeling somewhat better I took the tractor back to the shed to get some dry clothes. As I switched off the engine, I heard a whining noise. At first I thought it was just the ringing of the tractor motor still reverberating through my eardrums and up and down the corridors of my soul, but there it was again

A soft whining

and a few little yelps could be

heard from the far corner of the

shed.

As I approached the

sounds,

I realized that it was my beagle,

another of my best

friends;

and she was giving birth to four little

pups.

Trembling, I watched in awe.

Finally, wanting to take part in this

miracle,

I picked one up

and

held it close to my

heart.

It too was trembling

and still frightened by

birth.

I gently stroked the new born

pup

held it like a

cup

sipping a gentle kiss until it was

calm.

Stroking with sweet balm.

Mother looked on with caressing

eyes and tender concern.

In the midst of the tragedy of death, I was witnessing new birth and new beginnings. This episode would always have meaning for me, and its impact would grow through the years.

For the person of faith,

all endings hold the possibilities

of new beginnings,

for God meets each occasion of our

life with kindness.

The shaking of our foundations

sometimes leads us to build new,

stronger foundations and thereon

to erect greater edifices.

At the funeral service for Wendell, the minister said this tragedy was God's will. He said,

"We may not understand,

    but we must not question.

        We can only accept this as God's will."

Without knowing why at the time, this proclamation disturbed me. As a farm boy with my fingers and toes planted in the soil, I was much more at

    peace with growing crops,

    the storm, the rain, the rainbow

    of promise and security and hope,

    and the birth of little beagle puppies,

    these bathed my soul with

    healing balm, comfort,

    peace, and hope.

The idea of God taking the life of a young man in a cruel car accident was strange to my way of thinking. It did not resonate with my soul, but I simply did not have the words to express my feelings. Later my linguistic studies would reveal there are non-verbal and pre-reflective emotions, feelings, and thoughts that are virtually impossible to express in a one-to-one correlation to words and phrases. In my studies and experience I have learned faith is best defined as something other than a system of beliefs or creeds. I found that doctrines and creeds written by persons of another age did not correspond with my inner feelings and emotions. For me faith is the acknowledgement and embodiment of these feelings or moods of existence through which God is revealed as a relational God of kindness who is always with us. However, only as I studied the gentle life and tender teachings of sages like the Buddha, the Jewish prophets, Jesus, Martin Luther King, Jr., and Mother Teresa did I experience a sense of inner resonance and harmony. Through the prism of kindness these feelings and moods became my personal and private beliefs through which the presence of God and God's loving care were revealed.

This fits my relational hermeneutic of kindness that sees all things inter-connected and inter-related, seeing

>God in the world
>
>and for the world,
>
>in us
>
>and for us
>
>acting in kind saving ways.

Relational kindness recognizes individual freedom in the evolutionary process and sees individual self-determination and self-actualization as key to

understanding human existence. In the story of the Bible,

>God understands and cares for
>
>the ones who are suffering.
>
>God is in the relational process setting
>
>novel aims and purposes,

luring the struggling people of God in the fulfillment of these aims and purposes

>that are always good and loving.

Kindness reveals that God is not coercive in this relationship but persuasive and luring. God relates to the world from within as gentle persuasive activity. In Revelation, the last book of the Bible, we see this divine activity as the Spirit of God directing the new community in transforming ways.

To be sure John, like some Old Testament writers, does not always see this activity through the eyes of kindness, and we must respect his freedom in seeing things from his world view. At times he is almost totally consumed by suffering.

Yet, his use of creative images allows us to pick them up and interpret them through the lens of kindness that he sets before us in the introduction to Revelation in these words:

> "I pray that you will be blessed with kindness
>
> and peace from God,
>
> who is and was and is coming" (1:4).

To make sure we do not miss his concern for kindness, John closes his book with this prayer:

> "I pray that Jesus will be kind to you" (22:21).

John's lens of kindness invites us to flesh out his images of suffering, wrath, and vengeance with the kindness of God revealed in the tender teachings of the biblical writers; and especially for Christians, in the gentle life and tender teachings of Jesus we have in the four Gospels and the entire New Testament.

Relational Hermeneutic of Kindness: A Case Study

A hermeneutic of kindness allows us to interpret the biblical message in transforming ways, especially the difficult passages that seem to sanction wars of violence and aggression. And this is my hermeneutic for interpreting the whole Bible from Genesis to Revelation. I have especially found this hermeneutic of kindness helpful in understanding God and evil.

The woman Judge, Deborah, is a good place to see the struggle between violence and God's kindness. This Old Testament story is interpreted here with the relational hermeneutic of kindness as a way of showing how all difficult passages of the Bible can be interpreted.

Deborah and Barak

Encountering God

The stories of the Judges in the Old Testament have been difficult to understand. They are violent stories that portray God as a military king, commanding the destruction of the enemy, killing men, women, and children. The world view is best described as primitive and barbaric. Jewish and Christian interpreters need a hermeneutic that can balance these stories with a more worthy view of God.

The stories of the Judges are best understood as covenantal historical accounts. By covenant I mean that God formed a special relationship of kindness with Israel saying that I shall be your God and you shall be my people. By historical I mean that these covenant partners, God and the people of God, have precious stories of faith encounters that call for showing kindness to others.

God Is with Us

The story of Deborah and Barak answers one of the basic questions of our faith: Is God present with us or not? In answering this question, one must see how the people in these stories perceived God. Show me a people's culture and language and I will show you how they understand God. A common charge is that religious persons in all ages have tended to make God in their image, and on one level the Bible is a human book. Human words are always inadequate to express the mystery of the divine.

Yet, to affirm faith in God requires that we attempt to understand the nature of God and how God relates to us and to our world. When we seriously read the Bible, it quickly becomes obvious that we are reading more than a human book. On a very deep level the Bible is a divine book, and a heavenly Spirit shines through the human words. The story of Deborah and Barak is a channel through which the God of Israel speaks. It is the message that lies behind the messengers that is the focus. When we see this, we realize that as the heavens are higher than the earth, so God's thoughts and ways are higher than our words and actions (See Isaiah 55:8-9). More than any other book, the Bible counters and challenges our human ways of conceiving God.

The Call of Deborah and Barack

In the exploits of Deborah and Barak we witness the pattern that is repeated over and over in Israel's journeying with God toward the promised land. As they encounter strange cultures and new gods, they forget their God and worship idols. According to the writer of Judges, God punishes them by letting their enemies attack and defeat them. They turn back to God for help. God sends special leaders,

Deborah and Barak, to deliver them from their enemies. Israel is faithful for a while and then the pattern is repeated.

Deborah's and Barak's story is told in Judges, chapter 4 in prose and in chapter 5 in poetry or psalm format. In chapter 4 we learn that Deborah was a prophet and judge in Israel during a violent time when the people of God faced extinction from warfare. Not only was Deborah the only female judge, she was the first judge; and she set a judicial precedent for the twelve judges who came after her. Deborah was noted for her civil and social contributions. Before becoming a military leader, she sat "under the palm of Deborah" between Ramah and Bethel in the hill country of Ephraim, and the Israelites came up to her for judgment (4:4-5). Her respect as a civil judge enabled her to summon Barak and say to him that the God of Israel commanded him to summon an army for battle (4:6).

Deborah was a courageous and bold leader who could read the signs of the times. When she saw Jabin, the Canaanite king, marching across the land with nine hundred iron chariots, she went into action. She summoned Barak, an Israelite commander, and told him to gather his army of ten thousand. Deborah said that she would draw out the Canaanite army by the river Kishon and deliver them into his hands. Barak was hesitant and showed doubt saying that he would go if Deborah went with him. Deborah said, "I will surely go with you; nevertheless, the road on which you are going will not lead to your glory, for the Lord will sell Sisera into the hand of a woman." Listen to the way Israel sang praises to Deborah: *Awake, awake, Deborah! Awake, awake, utter a song! Arise, Barak, lead away your captive* (5:12). Then Deborah got up and led Barak and his army to Kedesh and won a great victory for Israel. Encouraging Israel to pray: "So perish all your enemies, O Lord!" (5:31).

An Unworthy View of God

From this Old Testament story, we see God present with Israel in her time of great need, and this is the main lesson we should learn from this story. Yet, this faith story is shaped through a particular world view that is best described as primitive and barbaric. God is portrayed like a military king commanding the destruction of the enemy, killing men, women, and children. As we interpret these violent stories today, we need to balance them with other more worthy views of God, for tragically, this view still controls many. Terrorist activity is often controlled by this view of God.

There is evidence in our sacred scriptures that the writers themselves struggled for some balance. When interpreting a difficult story like Deborah and Barak, I look for that evidence of balance, looking before and after our scripture selection in Judges 4:1-10.

A More Worthy View of God

This is what I found. In Judges 2:18, we read that God was with the judges and delivered them, for **God was "moved to pity** by their groaning." Here God is portrayed as having deep **compassion** and pity for the people of God. The Contemporary English Version of the American Bible Society translates the Hebrew word in this verse as **kindness**, translating the phrase as **"God was kind to Israel."**

Then in Deborah's song in Judges, chapter 5, one of the earliest songs recorded in scripture, we hear Israel singing about prosperity in Israel, "because you arose, Deborah, arose as a mother in Israel" (5:8). The Contemporary English Version translates this verse as **"Then Deborah took command, protecting Israel as a mother**

protects her children." This verse is the lens through which we should interpret Deborah's story.

These two verses in Judges 2:18 and 5:7, the bookends for bracketing Deborah's story, anticipate and will come to fruition in the theme of loving-kindness in the Psalms, a light to the nations in Isaiah, and the dawn of a new age that came in the tender teachings of Jesus. When reading about the military plundering and killing in Judges we need to keep this big unfolding picture in view. When writing this manuscript ISIS was bombing Paris and our world was saddened. If our desire for peace comes, we will have to seek peace and happiness not just for ourselves, but for all people of the world. That peace will come when we learn the lesson of kindness and mercy.

We are encouraged to see this growth and development in our understanding of God by the way Deborah's story is linked to Jesus. These lines from Deborah's song in chapter 5, verse 7 and verse 31b (Contemporary English Version) shows linkage with Luke's prophecy of the coming of Jesus. Judges 5:31b reads: "Let everyone who loves you shine brightly like the sun at dawn." Luke 1:77-78 expands this verse in these words: "By the tender mercy of God, the dawn from on high will break upon us, to give light to those who sit in darkness and in the shadow of death, to guide our feet into the way of peace" (Luke 1:77-78).

The tension between the views of God as a military king who commands and directs warfare and God as a mother tenderly showing kindness to her children is seen in the closing verse of Deborah's song in chapter 5, verse 31. "So perish all your enemies, O Lord! But may your friends be like the sun as it rises in its might." Like the composer of many of the Psalms, the writer of Judges is sure that his enemies are God's enemies, and as he wants to destroy his enemies, so he believes that God does also!

Our View of God Revealed in Jesus

Interpreters of the Bible have what the writer of Judges and the Psalms did not have. We have the full testimony of the Bible including the tender teachings of the prophets like Isaiah and Hosea. We have the gentle life and tender teachings of Jesus. The longer I live with these scriptures, especially the tender teachings of Jesus, the surer I am that God created out of chaos in order to share goodness and kindness with all people. From the gentle teachings of Jesus, I learn that God shapes creation with loving aims and purposes and spreads a banquet table before us. Then God invites us to the party. One strand of the story of the Exodus and the wilderness wanderings is that God sets the banquet table by providing manna from heaven.

Here is the image that shapes my view of God in these biblical stories: "Deborah arose as a mother in Israel" (Judges 5:7b.). This wisdom seed of seeing God like the tender care of a mother is planted in Deborah's song, it grows in the Psalms of Israel: "I have learned to feel safe and satisfied, just like a child on its mother's lap. People of Israel, you must trust the Lord now and forever" (Psalm 131), and comes to fruition in the prophets like Isaiah and Hosea and in the gentle teachings of Jesus: "Jerusalem, Jerusalem, . . . How often have I desired to gather your children together as a hen gathers her brood under her wings" (Luke 13:34). "Come to me, all you that are weary and are carrying heavy burdens, and I will give you rest. Learn from me, for I am gentle and humble in heart, and you will find rest for your souls" (Matthew 11:28-29).

God's loving kindness and tender care involves God as present in the world. Responsive love is compassionate suffering love as we can see in the judges. God suffers with the world. We know from personal experience that love is a sympathetic response from one person to another. True love feels what the other person is feeling, rejoicing in their joys and hurting with their pains. We would doubt that a mother loves her children if she were not aware of their feelings and if her feelings did not reflect their feelings.

As we experience God revealed in the story of Deborah and Barak interpreted through kindness, we find God rejoicing with us in our times of joy and weeping with us in our times of sorrow. In Deborah we see God protecting Israel as a mother protects her children (Judges 5:7b). This is responsiveness that is worthy of worship, prayer, and service. Our love of others is based on this responsive love we see in God. Our theology should reflect the awe and wonder of God being in the world, in us, and for us, holding us close as a mother holds her child in her lap and a mother hen gathers her brood under her wings.

Interpreting the Bible through the hermeneutic of kindness would help us elevate the role of women in Christian ministry, as well as equality among the sexes in our society and the business world. Ministry in all religions based on the Bible can no longer be shaped by old patriarchal views that never served the church well.

In seeking to understand Deborah and Barak, I sat quietly and read the book of Judges, the seventh book in the Old Testament, with the idea of drawing a profile of the judges. I came out with a striking picture. Only one of the 12 or 13 was a woman, but she was a daring prophetess and set a judicial precedent for her prophetic successors. We could wish for a more gentle spirit in Deborah, but she lived in a cruel and harsh land. Her story is preceded in 2:18 with a reference to the kindness of God toward Israel and ends with the description of Deborah as a judge who protected Israel as a mother cared for her children.

The longer I looked, the more I began to see Deborah and Barak as persons like you and me. They begin to look like leaders in our world today. There is a dark streak running through their decisions and actions. They are living through terribly complex times with the potential for total destruction and death from warfare, not unlike our own times. Yet they are not consumed and paralyzed by fear. Their faith in God is like a light shining in the darkness. Their courageous faith brings possibilities of hope. In this light I see their faces reflecting both the darkness and the light. Their strong countenance says to me that they are going to journey forward with God! Are we willing to do the same?

In painting the portraits of the judges, we get a glimpse of Israel's faith and see why these stories were used at all of Israel's great homecomings and at the launching of the Christian missionary movement in Acts. These stories told them some important truths about God: (1) God is purposeful, (2) God is powerful, (3) and God is personable, as personable as a Parent.

Relational Kindness and A Scientific World View

Whereas traditional theology saw God as passionless, as a perfect unchanging being, the hermeneutical task requires that we translate the message of God through our scientific world view. As a biblical theologian I affirm that God is the source of all truth. Integrity is a necessary element in an adequate biblical hermeneutic and requires the incorporation of scientific truth with a belief in God as the source of truth.

Faith stories lend themselves well to being interpreted through a relational hermeneutic of kindness that is balanced with scientific truth. Using relational kindness as my interpretive lens, enables me to say that God feels the feelings of all creation as responsive beneficiary, not benefactor only. A relational hermeneutic of kindness emphasizes the immanence of God, seeing God as synthesis of all our feelings and all feelings of the universe, and God is changed by this concrescence, this reciprocal activity of becoming through the unification of many feelings in which the many become one.

In biblical terms this is God loving the world and saving the world (see John 3:16, For God so loved the world). Concrescence in reference to persons is the act of becoming by unifying the possibilities presented by God's loving action in the world and for the world, in us and for us. Humans are partially created by their heredity and environment, what is given to them from the past, the present, and the lure of God; but humans exercise personal choice in the continuing process of becoming. Psychologically speaking, this is self-actualization.

Nurturing love is reciprocal in nature. God both gives and receives kindness and reciprocal kindness changes all coming into its warmth and glow. One touch of kindness makes us all kin.

In summary, the following are key concepts in my relational hermeneutic of kindness used in understanding God and the world.

(1) Relational. The way entities are interconnected and have relevance to one another. In the biblical message God, Jesus, and Spirit are interrelated as One in the experience of loving kindness in a cosmic community of becoming.

(2) Immanence. God is in all things. This is not pantheism which says that all things are God. Relational hermeneutics stresses that God is in all things as immanence, but God transcends all things as well, having creative power of persuasion, distinct from the universe.

(3) A reciprocal relationship of kindness between God and the world. It is as true to say that God is present in the world meeting each entity with kindness as to say that the world is present in God experiencing tender saving care. One of the main contributions of a relational hermeneutic of kindness is the change from a subject-object schema to subject-subject approach to interpretation. The biblical story as the revelation of God's kindness addresses the interpreter as subject. This reciprocal relationship of kindness transforms our lives, our ministry, and our world.

(4) Integrity of the natural order. For autonomous self-actualizing entities to emerge in the evolutionary ongoing process, it is necessary that the natural order be organized and regular, and therefore comprehensible to all evolving entities, including persons.

My hermeneutic of kindness adds to this "integrity of the natural order," insights from E. O. Wilson that humans have evolved with an innate need to relate to all of nature and to all other life forms. Two Greek words, βιος and φιλια are joined together to form "biophilia" and conveys love for all life forms. I have fleshed out Wilson's insightful and exciting theory of biophilia with the gentle teachings of the Bible.

(5) God as Spirit is the supremely related entity, One with the universe in creative responsive kindness.

(6) God's relational loving kindness is the guiding principle and ground of all ethical actions. In meeting each entity with kindness God gives intrinsic value that calls us to be kind to all other entities, human and non-human.

(7) Ecumenical Spirit: Kindness is a theme in most religions of the world. Buddha said often, "My teaching is kindness." For Christians Jesus is the best example of relational love, but this does not negate other religious leaders in all faith traditions. Also, Jesus' life and death, to have transforming power for us, must not violate the integrity of the natural order as defined in number four above. The miracle of the biblical stories is that they speak to people with all kinds of world views. I can sing hymns with bad theology and say the Apostles' Creed with its archaic language and do it as a sense of becoming one with the saints of the past and as a part of the communities of faith today that often have diverse views of Scripture. I can do this and still interpret the images through the gentle teachings of Jesus for myself, personally without excluding others.

The kindness of God revealed in the biblical writers and the gentle teachings of Jesus form the core of my faith and become the lens through which I interpret the biblical message. The remaining question is this: Does the hermeneutic of kindness show us how our life experiences should be interpreted and written? I humbly and prayerfully suggest that it does. Living God's loving kindness is the best way for us to overcome the violence that threatens to destroy us.

In making kindness my relational hermeneutic for interpreting the Bible and our life experience; including our understanding God and evil, some may feel that I am packing too much meaning in this one word, kindness. In my linguistic studies I have found that words do not have meaning, they have usage. Context determines how a word is used and what its meaning should be. For example, the word, bank, has many usages. If I say that I am taking a check to the bank, it has a clear meaning by the context in which I use it. If I say that he is fishing on the river bank, bank has a different meaning. If I say she made a perfect bank shot, bank has another usage and meaning.

My use of the word kindness broadens each time it is used to interpret the ways God relates to us in the biblical writers and in Jesus' gentle teaching and the ways we become kind in this adventurous journey into the mystery of God's relational ways. The adventure belongs to the adventurous, and I hope you will feel my excitement as you learn more about being kind to others.

A relational hermeneutic of kindness also fits the needs of our global pluralistic age. Many religions including Judaism, Islam, and Buddhism stress the theme of kindness. Isaac Bashevis Singer, author and Nobel Prize in Literature winner (1978) wrote,

> "Kindness, I've discovered, is everything in life."

Finally, this is my experience: God meets each occasion of my life with kindness and this inspires me to be kind to others, starting with my family and moving out in an ever-widening circle of kindness that is all-inclusive.

I may not be able to give all the kindness the world needs, but the world needs all the kindness I can give.

In the end, then, kindness is victorious.

Relational Kindness and Courageous Action

"Don't be afraid! I am the first, the last, and the living one." (Revelation 1:17-18)

Louise Penny has written over a dozen books set in a small Canadian village where friendship, loyalty, belonging and community are central characteristics. Her latest book is about the courage to be kind.

Much of the Bible was written to encourage the people of God to live faithfully with courageous actions for communal goodness. Kindness grounded in God's goodness to us and lived in the gentle lives and tender teachings of prophets, psalmists, and Jesus issues in kind actions. A hermeneutic of relational kindness requires the capacity to creatively move ahead with courageous action. This requires being centered in goodness, beauty, and love. Courage starts with persons and grows to include those around us. It is like a candle that warms all in its glow.

For kindness to issue in courageous action, the test of an adequate biblical hermeneutic, we must be able to recover the biblical vision of hope. Emily Dickinson, beautifully captures the vision of hope in her poem,

Hope Is the Thing with Feathers:

Hope is the thing with feathers

That perches in the soul

And sings the tune without the words

And never stops at all.

> And sweetest in the gale is heard—
>
> And sore must be the storm
>
> That could abash the little bird
>
> That kept so many warm.

Here is the shape of this vision of kindness as courageous action. **First**, our lives even the most perplexing parts, are woven into the fabric of God's kindness; and only God can see the design in its entirety. We see it only partially from the underside. Because God can see the grand vision of kindness in its entirety, this means it fits into heaven's point of view. If we lose sight of the hands that are weaving the mosaic, we are engulfed by meaninglessness. In the kind biblical teachers, we see the hands that do the weaving and the heart that shapes the design. To be held in kindness by those gentle hands is to know peace, security, joy, and hope.

Mother Teresa, like many saints of the past, was centered in courageous kindness. When asked how she could tirelessly go each morning to pick up the babies left on the streets of Calcutta and bring them to her clinic for care and healing, she said, "It is Jesus, really."

The **second** part of this courageous vision of kindness is this: "Don't be afraid! I am the first, the last, and the living one." (Revelation 1:17-18). The transforming presence of the living God is spiritually present in all kind actions giving courage to face our fears. Following the tender and loving way of Jesus casts out our fears.[78]

Kindness knows no boundaries. There is no room for narrow nationalism and misdirected denominationalism in this vision of

---

[78] See 1 John 4:18.

unhindered courageous kindness. To be sure, we are all different and we have many boundaries to cross; but the boundaries, including, national pride, religious differences, race, gender, economics, and the list grows daily, can all be overcome in this vision of courageous kindness.

Kindness is not only a unifying concept that holds the biblical message together, kindness also transcends the gap between the biblical world and today. Relational kindness makes the biblical message relevant today and helps to equip us for ministry in a broken world.

> As we send kindness into the world
>
> with wings,
>
> walls of prejudice fall down,
>
> sexual barriers are transcended,
>
> including persons of differing sexual preferences,
>
> anger and hatred are healed,
>
> poisoned water is made clean,
>
> and hungry children are fed.
>
> This is God's love for the world.
>
> God's kingdom is now present on earth as it is in heaven. God is now
>
> in the world in new ways
>
> and for the world
>
> in new tidal waves of saving loving kindness.

There is no better example of courageous kindness than Viktor Frankl. In 1959 Beacon Press brought out the English translation of Viktor Frankl's book, *Man's Search for Meaning*. The 1984 edition says in the preface that the book is now in its seventy-third printing in English and has sold almost two and a half million copies in English editions alone; it has also been translated into nineteen languages, including Japanese and Chinese. Dr. Frankl, a medical doctor, psychiatrist, and author of twenty-six books and literally hundreds of journal articles, was a survivor of the Nazi concentration camps in which his wife, mother, father, brother, and over six million of his larger family of Jewish people lost their lives. At the time of Frankl's death in 1997, the book had sold more than 10 million copies in 24 languages.

The first half of the book, *Man's Search for Meaning*, tells of Dr. Frankl's experiences in Auschwitz and other concentration camps. The second half of the book is an introduction to logotherapy which are lessons learned in the first part. When asked to put his therapeutic system of psychoanalysis in a "nutshell," Dr. Frankl said it was an almost hopeless task, after all, he had written twenty books in his German language to explain his system of counseling. And here I am trying to explain it in a few pages. But, **as an illustration of the power of healing kindness it is worth the effort.**

Logotherapy is based on two Greek words, λογος, (noun, logos,), which denotes meaning, and θεραπευω (verb, therapy), which denotes healing. —A concern at the heart of my hermeneutic of kindness. There are three interconnected concepts in logotherapy: (1) the freedom of will, (2) the will to meaning, and (3) the meaning of life. In its search for meaning, logotherapy is less retrospective, i.e., looking to the past, and less introspective, looking within the psyche, than Freud and Adler. Logotherapy looks to the future. Dr. Frankl often asked his patients, suffering from a multitude of torments great and small, "Why do you not commit suicide?" From their answer he found the guidelines for his counseling. One person may speak of love for a child, another may speak of a talent to be used, and still another may speak of a lingering memory. To weave a pattern of meaning and responsibility from these slender threads of a broken life is the challenge of logotherapy. According to logotherapy, each life has meaning and the drive to find meaning is the primary motivational force in life.

I find the three concepts of logotherapy compatible to my vision of courageous kindness and a fertile seed bed for learning how to deal with all acts of unkindness. The emphasis on "will" is illuminating for the way our Bible closed its vision: "The Spirit says let the one who is thirsty, Come. Let the one willing (θελων) take the water of life freely" (Revelation 22:17). This could be phrased: Let the one who wills meaning come to the God of kindness and find life's ultimate meaning. Life is not controlled by fate, but by transforming kindness.

Λογος and σοφια as used in the Bible are supremely the revelation of meaning and wisdom that was actualized in gentle teachings and therapeutic actions of courageous kindness. Jesus found this meaning under the shadow of the cross and indeed on the cross through self-transcendence. Suffering ceases to be the same in the moment it is transcended. Jesus lived and taught self-denial as the way to find the meaning of life and on the cross, he died for this truth.

When Jesus began to speak about his impending suffering and death, Peter took Jesus aside and asked him to stop talking like that. Jesus replied, "You are not talking like God. Then Jesus gathered his disciples close and said, 'If any of you want to be my followers, you must forget about yourself. You must take up your cross and follow me. If you want to save your life, you will destroy it. But if you give up your life for me and for the good news, you will save it'" (Mark 8:31-35). Self-transcendence comes through self-denial and taking up a larger transformational cause.

So, let me use Frankl's interconnected concepts of meaning as the framework for understanding courageous kindness. Frankl's kindness was therapeutic for him and for those who received his kindness. The New Testament Greek word is θεραπευω. We get the English word, therapeutic, from this Greek word found in Revelation 13:3, 12. The word refers to the most evil of characters---the beast who rises up from the sea and curses God and all who believe in God. John says that this beast looked as though it had been fatally wounded but now was healed (εθεραπευθη). And as if this evil beast were not enough, John adds a second one who comes up out of the ground and works for the first beast who was healed (εθεραπευθη). Perhaps John is using the two beasts to show the comprehensive nature of evil that affects both land and sea. Could there be a more apt description of suffering in all ages?

The intriguing thing about John's use of this Greek word is that he moves from the power of the beast to curse God and all things that God brings into being to the call for wisdom to understand the beastly evil. John who thinks in Hebrew and writes in Greek reaches into his vocabulary bag and pulls out the magic word: σοφια. "You need σοφια to understand the beast" (13:18). In Jewish wisdom literature, Sophia, a feminine aspect of God, was used to balance the logos, the masculine aspect of God. With wisdom as our guide let us first look more deeply at the concept of "freedom of will" in Viktor Frankl's vision of kind actions.

The Freedom of Will

To understand the centrality of this concept for Dr. Frankl and for our hermeneutic of kindness, we must remember that he discovered the importance of this concept in the Nazi prison camps where you would think he had no freedom and no will to exercise. Those conditions were similar to John's situation in exile where he was hearing of the martyrdom of the followers of Jesus. Dr. Frankl is not speaking of freedom from conditions, but freedom to take a meaningful stand on whatever conditions one faces. Humans have the unique capacity to detach themselves from any situation however horrible it may be. Frankl built his whole system of logotherapy on this foundational principle: the search for meaning is life's primary motivational force.

The Gospel writers of the New Testament, like Frankl, saw the importance of the freedom of will. The noun and verb, θελημα, θελω, usually translated as "will" and "to will," occur about 275 times in the Greek New Testament, the majority occurring in the Gospels. The words are seldom used in Revelation but do occur most notably in 22:17: "The Spirit says let the one who is thirsty, Come. Let the one willing (θελων) take the water of life freely. "John understood that we have the freedom to will, i.e., make our own choices. Each of the letters to the seven Churches closes with the plea to "listen to what the Spirit, the risen Jesus, is saying to them" (Revelation chapters 2 and 3). He invites them to pray, worship, and listen to the "good news" (14:6) so that they can will (θελων) what is best.

Now, let us look further at Frankl's second concept of logotherapy, the will to meaning.

Will to Meaning

Frankl believed that each person is responsible for finding meaning in life. The counselor cannot give meaning to a person, but each person has the capacity to will meaning. The counselor does offer what he or she has found convincing. You cannot persuade others to will meaning if you are not convinced yourself that there is meaning in life. When asked by the editors of *Who's Who in America* to explain his life in a few lines, Frankl wrote, "I have seen the meaning of my life in helping others to see in their lives a meaning." Frankl had made the conscious decision to be in a helping profession and willing his life in that direction he found the meaning of his life. And he found it in the midst of suffering in the Nazi death camps as he showed kindness for the medical needs of those suffering around him.

Logotherapy says that we may not be able to choose the cards life deals us, but we can choose how to view and arrange the cards, which to discard and which to keep for a winning hand. We can choose our reaction to life and its complex set of problems. Rather than being pushed by inner drives and external forces, we can be pulled by meaning. Meaning fulfillment requires decision-making.

Jesus found meaning in his life, as the prophets before him did, as he actualized the creative loving kindness of God in his life, and he never stopped trying to help others find that same meaning. Jesus expressed this as a divine compulsion: "I must be about my Father's business. Jesus cannot give us meaning, but he is a role model of how we can find meaning in life by self-transcendence of our suffering and actualizing God's kindness that transforms our suffering. We are not talking about meaning in the abstract sense; meaning is specific for each person and must be discovered by each person in a given time and place. For Jesus this was a daily choice of showing kindness to the suffering. To live in God's kindness is to live in the power field of God's Spirit and to model our life after the kind leaders and teachers who have touched our lives and continue to bless us.

A word of caution needs to be added here. I am not speaking of the popular "power of positive thinking." Will to meaning cannot be commanded or ordered or demanded. Life's meaning is found by having faith in God's aim and purpose for all humanity. John's closing prayer for following the kindness of Jesus is a desire for the kindness of God to flow in the lives of the followers of Jesus in his circle of Churches (See Revelation 22:21, CEV). Will to meaning is elicited by elucidating meaning itself. The crucial question is does life have meaning?

The Meaning of Life

Viktor Frankl had an unshakable faith in an unconditional ultimate meaning in life. Not even the horrors of the holocaust could shake his faith in life's ultimate meaning. According to his system of logotherapy, we can discover this third concept, the meaning of life, in three primary ways: (1) by creating a work or performing deeds of kindness; (2) by experiencing beauty and encountering love; and (3) by the attitude we take toward tragic events we cannot change like unavoidable suffering. Let me personally expand on Frankl's three primary ways of finding meaning. First, we find meaning by giving creative value to the world and to people we encounter. For fifty years my sermons, counseling, my whole ministry of kindness was my gift to others, and I found meaning for my life through ministry.

Second, we find meaning through the experiential values we take from the world and from Christian community. My vision of courageous kindness is fueled by the beauty I experience in God's good creation. I took a vacation with Beth, my wife, in San Francisco and Yosemite. While in Yosemite, we saw giant sequoias that were over 3,000 years old.

Meaning is also gained through significant encounters with people we love. Vacations are special because they are shared with people we love. Our encounters with people we serve have special meaning as well, and that is their creative gift to us.

Dr. Frankl's third way of finding meaning, attitudinal values, is most difficult to understand. This highest of values comes from the attitude we take to predicaments we can't change like unavoidable suffering. We have not faced the suffering of the holocaust, but we all face the unavoidable pain, grief, and sorrow of growing old, and sooner or later we must all die. We can rail against this, drown the pain and fear in alcohol and drugs or we can will to accept this aging process with an attitude of dignity and grace. Aging, like all forms of suffering, can have ultimate meaning if it changes one for the better. For the Christian this attitude is called faith.

Dr. Frankl's faith was grounded in the God of the Old Testament. He closed his book, *The Will to Meaning*, with the song of Habakkuk who displayed an unconditional trust in ultimate meaning:

> Even though the fig trees have no fruit
>
> and no grapes grow on the vines,
>
> even though the olive crop fails
>
> and the fields produce no grain,

> even though the sheep all die
>
> and the cattle stalls are empty,
>
> I will be joyful and glad,
>
> because the Lord God is my savior.
>
> The Sovereign Lord gives me strength.
>
> He makes me sure footed as a deer
>
> and keeps me safe on the mountains (3:17-19).

John's vision of courageous kindness carries Habakkuk's triumphant hymn to new heights in his anthems of praise in places like Revelation 7:17 where he speaks of the shepherd who will lead them to streams of living water, invoking Psalm 23. Also, in 4:8b, "Holy, Holy, Holy is the Lord, the all-powerful God, who was and is and is coming." "Our Lord and God, you are worthy to receive glory, honor, and power. You created all things, and by your decision they are and were created" (Revelation 4:11). "Then I heard all beings in heaven and on the earth and under the earth and in the sea offer praise. Together all of them were saying, 'Praise, honor, glory, and strength forever and ever to the one who sits on the throne and to the Lamb!'" (Revelation 5:13).

John knew that by faith in Jesus (Revelation 2:19; 14:12; 19:10) the believer is exalted to a new level of meaningful existence with Jesus and the saints around the throne. In communal kindness we find the ultimate meaning of life. In communion with God life is never short of meaning. To God be the glory!

Concluding Meditation

Wishing to encourage her young son's progress on the piano, a mother took her boy to a Paderewski concert. After they were seated, the mother spotted a friend in the audience and walked down the aisle to greet her. Seizing the opportunity to explore the wonders of the concert hall, the little boy rose and eventually explored his way through a door marked "NO AMITTANCE." When the house lights dimmed and the concert was about to begin, the mother returned to her seat and discovered that her son was missing. Suddenly, the curtains parted, and spotlights focused on the impressive Steinway on stage. In horror, the mother saw her little boy sitting at the keyboard, innocently pecking out "Twinkle, Twinkle, Little Star." At that moment the great piano master made his entrance, quickly moved to the piano, and whispered in the boy's ear, "Don't quit. Keep playing." Then leaning over, Paderewski reached down with his left hand and began to fill in a bass part. Soon his right hand reached around to the other side of the child and he added a running obligato. Together, the old master and the young novice transformed a frightening situation into a wonderfully creative experience. And the audience was mesmerized.

Whatever your situation in life, God comes to sit beside you and whisper, "Don't quit. Keep praying. You are not alone." Then reaching tender arms around you, says, "Together we will transform the broken patterns into a masterwork of creative art." God is like an artist creating newness; God is creating a new heaven and a new earth where there will be no more death, suffering, crying, or pain. These things of the past are transformed! (Revelation 21:3-4).

John's courageous vision of a new heaven and a new earth is marked by kindness and peace---his prayer from beginning to end. Kindness and peace ground John's vision of a new heaven and a new earth in reality in the seven churches. For John there was a risk that the passing of the old heaven and old earth would not result in kindness. In prolonged persecution kindness can easily melt into hatred and a desire for vengeance. Even John's vision springing from his collective unconsciousness and his personal consciousness wavers between a desire for vengeance on his enemies and a prayer for Jesus' kindness. This is not a new pattern for the Bible. One sees this same pattern in the lament Psalms. Indeed, the whole Old Testament as the story of God's people, as the biography of God, is marked by bondage, suffering, and deliverance.

This is the dilemma of the biblical scholar: If the Bible is the biography of God and God's people, how can one speak of such mystery? John recognized this difficulty when he was moved to silence before the throne of God. In poetic language this is how I understand John's dilemma.

Silence Before God

Hello God, I have come to talk with you again.

A vision left its images planted in my soul while I was sleeping.

In restless sleep I walked up and down the aisles of my seven churches.

And this is what I saw.

I saw people in despair and grief, suffering and wailing.

I heard them pray, how long, O God, how long?

This is what I said to them.

Friends hear the words of God that you might endure your pain.

Let the kindness of God be your song of hope.

Words were spoken, songs were sung.

And there was silence before God!

Ansel Adams once said, "When words become unclear, I shall focus with photographs. When images become inadequate, I shall be content with silence." All great artists grope for words and images to express mystery.

John's vision in Revelation is a work of great art. In seeking to express his vision he used powerful words of God from his sacred scriptures. When words failed him, he used transforming metaphorical images like rainbow, lamb, shepherd, and the sparkling throne of God in heaven. In the radiant glow of the throne John was content with silence: "When the lamb opened the seventh seal there was silence in heaven for half an hour" (Revelation 8:1).

In seeking to understand John's vision of courageous kindness in Revelation, we are confronted with deep mystery. Our search for meaning began with mystery and it ends in mystery. This is as it should be, for all deep truth must be represented by mystery shading into myth. The biblical story in Genesis of God walking in the Garden of Eden with Adam and Eve to the new heaven and earth with streams of life-giving waters where God wipes all tears from all eyes (Revelation 7:17) is told with mysterious mythic language.

My hermeneutic of relational kindness seeks to make a contribution to this search for meaning. At the heart of this vision is the faith that kindness transforms suffering. So we close this book with the Bible's closing prayer and our prayer: "I pray that Jesus will be kind to all of you" (Revelation 22:21).

Summary

In summary, I have proposed that Kindness is a good hermeneutic for interpreting the Bible. I have used kindness as a unifying biblical and societal concept that seeks to elucidate the relational nature of reality, emphasizing becoming rather than static existence of all things. The Bible is about relationships from Genesis to Revelation where everything is continually changing with the evolutionary energy of kindness. In the first book of the Bible we have a beautiful mythic-poetic account of God walking in the new Garden of Eden with Adam and Eve and in the last book of the Bible the old earth and the old heaven are passing away and the new earth and new heaven are continually being born.

The old is not an enduring unchanging substance; it is continually experienced as new events. The mythic poetry of Genesis is well suited to express evolving life within the sphere of good and evil.

As the story of good and evil unfolds in human history, a hermeneutic is needed to unravel the mystery. For me, the theme of kindness is the best lens through which to understand this mystery and learn how to cope with evil. The ultimate test of a theological or philosophical system is does it ring true to our experience. As a minister in a local Church for over 50 years I saw how the gentle teachings of the biblical writers slowly but surely change our lives and our world.

Gentle teachings are especially suited as a hermeneutic, a prism through which we view and interpret the Bible. God's kindness transforms life, creating wonder and stimulating creative actions of kindness. This is my hermeneutic from Alpha to Omega, from beginning to end. The kindness of God shines throughout the Bible. And that kindness has transforming energy. Here is the heartbeat of my hermeneutic:

> The kindness we show to ourselves, our family,
>
> and to all living things
>
> is the greatest healing force in the world.

Here are the elements I have found that define kindness. **First,** kindness is grounded in the covenant God made with God's people. In the covenant with us God relates in kindness. God meets each event in life with kindness. In our covenant with God we commit to being kind to others as God is kind to us. The fundamental idea in covenant is connectiveness and counterbalance. Kindness is the connecting bridge from God to us and us to God and others. For Christians, Jesus is a good example of that bridge and of bridge building. The bridge of kindness is balanced and can be entered from both sides.

Jesus is a path that marks a journey toward God, and not the only way. When the Gospel of John describes Jesus as the way to God, this should not be seen as an exclusive statement. The words, path, road, and journey are not perfect. I prefer Saint Augustine's image of God as a circle whose center is everywhere, and whose circumference is nowhere.

Second, kindness is healing. Kindness heals suffering, grief, and sorrow. Kindness is wrapping arms of love and care around the hurting. Freud in a letter to Jung said that in all the healing he had witnessed, love was always present.

God is best conceived as kindness, with infinite patience drawing all into a redemptive relationship of beauty, goodness, and love. This is

God present with us giving value to our lives and relationships, all of which are grounded in God's kindness. Our potential becomes actual in this phase of social solidarity where we grow with God and each other in kindness.

The hermeneutic of kindness seeks to interpret these tender feelings and actions that slowly operate by love. The hermeneutical message does not focus on the future. Its power lies in the transformation of the present, an immediacy that does not seek to rule and judge but finds its own joy in present zestfulness.

Kindness is reciprocal in this sense. As God's eternal goodness is actualized in our lives and relationships it becomes immortalized, passing from earth to heaven and back into our lives and our world of suffering and woe. God understands and suffers with us. As we join our love energies with God and with each other, kindness is redemptive and healing.

Interpreters of the Bible today have the full testimony of the Bible including the tender teachings of the prophets like Isaiah and Hosea. We have the gentle life and tender teachings of Jesus. The longer I live with these scriptures, especially the tender teachings of Jesus, the surer I am that God created out of chaos in order to share goodness and kindness with all people. From the gentle teachings of Jesus, I learn that God shapes creation with loving aims and purposes and spreads a banquet table before us. Then God invites us to the party. In celebrating kindness, we live eternally.

My hermeneutic of kindness has not been an argument with God. Its concern has been more along the lines of Walt Whitman's advice in the 1855 preface to *Leaves of Grass:*

Argue not concerning God. . ... re-examine all you have been told at church or school or in any book, dismiss whatever insults your soul. . .

My goal has been a healing universal kindness that breaks down cultural and religious barriers that divide and exclude, even when they are found in the Bible and our religious institutions. In this renewal of kindness, the many can become one in a peace that passes understanding.

Kindness Training Exercise

This book has been about relational kindness. Relational is key. Life is about relationships from birth till death. Relational kindness comes naturally in family and community and flows in personal ways. Yet, mindfully setting aside times to meditate on how we can better show kindness can help us become more sensitive and responsive to others within our everyday circles and move to include all persons.

Find a quiet time each day to prayerfully think about what you desire for your family and yourself:

*   To be safe and secure

*   To be happy and at peace

*   To have good health

*   To be free from fear

*   To have fun times for all in your family

*   To be kind to each other and all people, animals, and all living things

*   Showing kindness is a healing activity. Consciously think kind thoughts throughout your daily activity and feel those energies flowing to others.

APPENDIX A: Jesus and God Consciousness

The heart of this relational hermeneutic is Jesus and his gentle Galilean teachings. Throughout there are references to Jesus' unique God consciousness, a concept first popularized by the philosopher, Fredrick Schleiermacher. The concept has been used by many theologians since Schleiermacher, often with increasing richness. As used in this book "God-consciousness" refers to Jesus learning to incorporate each moment of his life in an experience of God's life. This creative rhythmic responsiveness brought a fusion of human and divine love. Thus, in Jesus' words and actions we see and feel God acting in tender and caring ways that nothing be lost. Practicing kindness in our words and actions can lead to a greater awareness of God's presence within us.

The psychiatrist C.G. Jung is known for his work on archetypes, the personal consciousness, and the collective unconscious. For Jung the collective unconscious is the deeper layer of consciousness that lies under the personal consciousness and does not derive from personal experience; it is not a personal acquisition but is inborn. It is collective in the sense that it is not individual but universal. Recently, human consciousness has been at the center of much psychiatric study focusing on new understandings of the human brain.

Today scientific theories are moving consciousness outside of the human brain. Giulio Tononi and his colleagues at the University of Wisconsin-Madison have the goal of understanding how the brain generates consciousness. They are using state of the art brain scanners and the latest computer programs to produce torrents of information on brain function. Tononi's quiet reflection after amassing this information is that each split second of awareness is a unified experience that is completely new and different from any experience before or after it.

Tononi's theory defines consciousness as the capacity of a person or any system to connect and use information. Each moment of existence has the potential of playing out in a limitless number of ways. Yet, the instant an experience is integrated and gels, the options vanish. The next moment brings new possibilities, new options, and new experience forming consciousness. The many options produce the one new experience. So Tononi's theory is information +integration=experience (consciousness).

Integration is what makes every conscious experience a unified whole. These two concepts: information and integration describe consciousness. If this equation is correct, then Tononi untethers the theory of consciousness from the physical brain. Silicon chips integrating information zooming around the World Wide Web produces consciousness. It is interesting to see that ancient religions and current panpsychism says the same thing. Other scientists today say that the only systems that we know that fulfill Tononi's theory are biological.

My own belief is that the possibility of consciousness is inherent in the fabric of reality as God's initial love aims and purposes for an evolving universe. Consciousness is woven into the very fabric of cosmos as possibilities, as information to be experienced by emergent creatures.

Consciousness is grounded in God best known as creative relational kindness. As God calls creation out of chaos over eons of time, the evolving creation is conducive to the formation of human consciousness. As God's novel love aims and purposes were experienced and unified, consciousness emerged. The ethical quality of consciousness and the presence of moral law in many cultures support this view. Thus, the origin of consciousness is primarily in the Divine and secondarily in humans. Since God's Spirit is in all things, then consciousness can be experienced in varying degrees at many levels of evolution.

Jesus' gentle Galilean glories, his gentle teachings, are unique in that Jesus became totally obedient to God's call. In each succeeding act of obedience, Jesus became more conscious of God's love aims and purposes until he became fully God conscious. Jesus' consciousness was God's consciousness, and both Jesus and God were changed in the process; thus, he could say as he faced the cross, God and I are one (See John 17). Divine consciousness is greater than that experienced by Jesus.

Jesus' consciousness was the totality of all his sensory experiences. He was aware of his religious past, how God was revealed in the consciousness of the prophets like Isaiah. Seeing God revealed in the prophets opened the way for Jesus to become God conscious. Jesus received the information of God's actions in the world from the past, preserved in his sacred scriptures and buried in his consciousness, integrated this information into his experience of God, and became more fully God conscious with each self-actualization. This is in harmony with Luke's understanding of Jesus when he wrote, "Jesus increased in wisdom and stature, in favor with God and persons" (Luke 2:52). Also, the writer of Hebrew says that Jesus learned obedience (Hebrews 5:8).

Gentleness as actualized by Jesus is like an archetype of consciousness, rooted in the nature of God and layered in many religions from ancient times. The Hebrew/Greek words for gentleness could be called archetypal words for gentleness set forth in the secrets of Jesus' consciousness in glorious images that can inspire and transform, making gentleness accessible to every believing heart.

These images of gentleness be they Jewish, Christian, or Buddhist are mysteriously, richly intuitive. In their archetypal nature these images of kindness often covey mythic qualities as they are associated with the birth of Jesus. As in Luke 1:78-79, where the Gospel writer says about the birth narratives, God's love and kindness will shine on us from on high.

Jesus incarnated these images of kindness and the early Christians were gripped by these images, as can be seen in the New Testament literature of the early church. I am afraid that for the church today these archetypal images of gentleness have been worn smooth by usage and have become superficial and banal, replaced by correct belief set in the concrete of creeds. Thus, dogma takes the place of gentle consciousness and the gentle Jesus is replaced by the ways of Caesar. Gentleness, if not cast out of the psyche into cosmic space, lies buried in the layers of personal consciousness, waiting for a reawakening.

Having ceased to think theologically, the contemporary church doesn't have the remotest conception of the treasure buried in these human vessels. When the church ceases to think seriously about these images of gentleness and how the Trinity reveals the love and kindness of God coming to save us (See Titus 3:4), the church is stripped of mystery, its walls collapse, exposing the evil winds of the world.

The modern church members enlightened consciousness leads him/her to look elsewhere for what has been lost in the archetypal image of collective kindness. The success of the mega-church is due to its effective use of theatrical imagery and pabulum feed theology that satisfies the restlessness of heart and mind.

Meanwhile, the archetypal image of gentleness that Jesus incarnated in his God-consciousness remains an unrealized dream. Reawakening this gentle conscious is the route to zestful love, joy, and peace, the harmony of harmonies.

Jesus' God-consciousness is a model of how the world might be. It came to fruition in Jesus' consciousness after being shaped over time with the sacrifice of many including the sacrifice of the prophets of Israel as told in the Old Testament; it was born more fully in the life and gentle teachings of Jesus, his sacrificial death on the cross, and his glorious resurrection.

Without the inner glow of this God-consciousness there would be no real sight or the light that unifies human consciousness. Go and seek that light!

APPENDIX B: Religious Poetry and Hermeneutic

I chose a prose/poetic format for this book as a way of imaging God as kindness and understanding the way God meets each entity of the world with kindness. Poetry opens us to new ways of seeing and hearing others while at the same time opening our hearts to more tender ways. We are at a critical juncture in human relations and world relations. Widespread violence based on race and religion is threatening life on our planet. Our future may well depend on our growing in kindness. A union of science and the humanities is needed for a well-rounded hermeneutic for interpreting our religious faith. I offer the poetry below as my attempt to unite these disciplines.

Be Kind

As a linguist,
I have seen how words are powerful
and the precursor to action---
Hostile words often lead
to hostile actions.
Kindness is like honey---
Sweet to the taste
and healing to the soul.
Taste and see that God is
good,
loving,
and kind.

Be kind to one another.

Part 2

As a poet,
how do you spend your day?   I am kind.

With Breaking News all day,
how do you focus?   I am kind.

In becoming the voice of the little ones,
how do you remain sincere?   I am kind.

In an age of global disbelief,
how do you center on God?   I am kind.

The House that Kindness Built

On the serene hillside it stands,
the house that kindness built.
The windows of faith, hope, love, joy, and peace
radiate light for your adventure.
The path is narrow and winding;
but if you, traveler, stay centered
in worship, prayer, and mindfulness.
You will come at last to
the house that kindness built.

God is the One unifying actuality.

In seminary I studied
devotional classics.
Visited Thomas Merton
at Gethsemane Monastery
and saw the importance of a contemplative lifestyle.

Fifty years later
I still go quietly
into nature
as my hermitage
to meditate on reality.

Nature speaks to me
and UNLIKE much human activity
the message is
logical and coherent.

In nature all is integrally related.
This revelation is universally applicable to daily living.
Poetry exhibits this reality
of one in all
and all in one.

In my religious poetry
God is the One unifying actuality.
God evolves in relationship
with the evolving world.

Religion, science,
sociology, and psychology,
Indeed, all the ologies
are fused into poetic thought
with alpenglow-ology.
Alpenglow poetic imagination
gives birth
to what is unrealized,
in human terms,
In the womb of nature.
Awake from sleep,
oh my soul.
Go out into God's universe---
Hear the call of nature.
See beauty.
Shake the world.

The Meaning of Life

One of the most asked questions around the world—
What is life all about?
We especially ask,
What is the meaning of my suffering?

The questions are so many:
Why did my child die in a school shooting?
Why was my son killed in this terrible war?
Why was my family lost in a car accident?

Why?

As a minister I had to answer these questions.
From the slender threads of broken lives
I tried to weave patterns of meaning.

In asking why
one can find a

How?

Here is the how:
All life is precious, has value,
and holds potential meaning
under any circumstance.

We cannot always choose
what life deals to us,
but we can choose our reaction
to what is dealt.

Here is the path of how,
leading to healing:
Find someone to listen,
comfort, console.
Focus with that person
on the precious moments you still have.

Center on goodness, grace, and love.

If you cannot find that person,
go gently into nature
and be still.

Nature will speak to you.
Nature has healing
and restoring powers.

Where is God?

Understanding God!
I am always trying to find God.
What is God like?
What shape?
Where is God, anyway?

The prophet, Isaiah said,
God's thoughts
are not our thoughts,
and our ways are not God's ways.

I wake everyday thinking,
Today I will find God.
I see a glorious sunrise,
My soul trembles in awe—
Is this God?

I touch a dimple on
my grandchildren's sweet face,
a brief smile as warm as
the earth's sun rise—
is this God?

After driving the grandkids to school
I take a long walk in the Chugach mountains.
Wild flowers and chickadees
brighten my way—
Is this God?

I remember Jesus' words:
God cares for the birds of the air
and the flowers of the fields.
God cares for you and me.

All day I walk at the edge of knowing
looking, longing, touching,
in beauty, goodness, and love, looking for God.
Maybe I will never know for sure where God is, but
this day feels like an answer!

One touch of nature's soul
makes us whole,
makes us feel—
In one glorious sunrise
we will all heal.

Kindness is All Inclusive

I have been accused of reducing the Bible
to one theme---the message of kindness.

I confess,
I am guilty as charged.

I was nurtured in kindness
by my parents and grandparents,
my extended family and faith family.

In my study and church ministry,
I was nurtured in kindness
by professors, deacons, elders,
and saintly church members.

In these reciprocal loving relationships
kindness flowered,
offering the balm of healing perfume,
sweet smelling incense.

Kindness became my heartbeat—
My eyes, ears, hands, and feet.

My theology and creed is this:
God meets each moment of
our lives with kindness,
and calls us to be kind to others.

Our theology and creeds express
the heartbeat of our living faith
found in the Bible stories
and practiced in communal living.

The Bible itself was written
over a 1,000-year period
from stories told and retold
before being written down.

These stories were shaped
by the culture in which
they were told and written down.

It is helpful when we read the Bible today
to ask two questions:
What did the story mean when it was written?
What does the story mean today?

These two questions are the structure
of my hermeneutic of kindness.

Kindness Blessing

May kindness be in our thoughts, making them good and loving.
May kindness be in our eyes,
leading us to see what is just in life.
May kindness be in our hands and feet
so that we may be
of service to others.
May kindness be in our whole being –
Making us one with God and the universe.

I don't know how to define kindness,
but I know for sure when I feel it.

Kindness is the language
known around the world.

Kindness is Everything

If you want to be happy.
    Be kind to yourself.

If you want others to be happy.
    Be kind to them.

If you want nature to be happy.
Be kind to birds, flowers, bees, and trees.

If you want to be happy
    Be kind.

Does God Break the Rules?

Some days it does seem that God
who makes each beautiful day
and meets it with kindness,
also,
breaks the rules and
takes life at will—
babies who die in the womb,
children who drown in swollen streams,
youth by the gang-banger's gun,
adults with broken dreams.
Some days it is as though God walks
through the flower fields,
and talks—
don't do this
and don't do that
whacking with a switch
the flowers in their prime!
Leaving us to pick up the bleeding hearts.
We all know the moonless midnight of the soul.

I wrote the poem below to remind me of the light of God's goodness:

Birds and Flowers---

Jesus spoke of the birds of the air
and flowers of the field.

Seeing and hearing birds,
the brain makes melodic music.
My heart is thankful
for the graceful beauties
who dance upon the wind
and make the music of the spheres.
Seeing and smelling flowers,
my soul is enraptured.
Cupping the flower,
my spirit breathes,
"Thank you for the grace
of your blossoms,
the sweetness of your breath,
and for sprinkling heaven's colors,
along my earthly path."

Considering how God cares
for the birds and flowers,
I believe and trust
in God's care for me.

Gift of Kindness

Joyfully we seek you, God of kindness.
You are always blessing---
birds singing a sweet melody
the summer sun caressing the flowers.

Let us taste the gift of your kindness---
March together arm in arm
heart to heart.
Kindness is the language
Known and heard around the world.

Sing the song of victory—
Kindness to all.
The triumphant song of eternity.

I wrote this little poem for all Sages of Sight,
my minister friends, elders, deacons,
and all committed to goodness and love:

Oh, sage of sight

hold the light
that keeps hope shining.

Sing, Oh my soul,
sing the song of kindness,
sure and strong.

One of the most cherished chapters in the Bible
    is First Corinthians 13,
        known as the love chapter.

Verse 4 is the heartbeat of this love poem:
"Love is patient; love is kind;
love is not envious or boastful or arrogant."

Almost every translation,
including the King James Version,
equates love and kindness.

As we go through this day
may we join love and kindness
in our attitudes and actions.

Kindness heals both the ones giving
and the ones receiving.
Let us go and be kind.

The Shape of Love
(I John 4:7)

We				
must	love	when	other	We become
love	comes from	we each		God's
each other	God	love		children.

My Shepherd

When I walk through fields of wild flowers
I know God is my shepherd.
When I wade in gurgling streams
filled with wild salmon
God refreshes my faith in goodness.

When I walk through dark Alaska nights,
God is leading me.
God is with me and
I am not afraid.

My fly rod is
a shepherd's rod.
It makes me feel safe.
Grace fills my cup
until it overflows.

Each day of my life
Kindness
and love is with me.

In God's house of nature
I will live
forever.
(based on Psalm 23) —

Adam and Eve

Adam and Eve, the first romance couple,
You have been placed in many boxes:
> myth
>> history,
>>> art,
>>>> literature,
>>>>> poetry.

        Come out of your boxes
        and become models
        of reconciliation and love.
        Teach us how to live as one.

        We are born to love.
Life's meaning is found in loving another person.

Galilean Images

In Jesus' life and teachings
tender love energies appeared
that slowly transform our lives
and our world.

This gentle life
evokes the best in human nature:
The gentle mother,
the baby Jesus,
the lowly servant teacher.

The message of kindness and love
all without force or coercion
yet with the authority
of heaven's stamp of approval.

Galilean images
dreams
of an unrealized world.

Contemplation of nature

Contemplation of nature
is the first step
in knowledge of God.

Nature is like a mirror
in which we look
to see the face of God;

Jesus preached the Gospel
not only in word,
but also in images
of birds and flowers,
crops and fields.

Jesus' gentle life spoke
and his kind words acted.
Ordinary words with
extraordinary meaning.

Each spoken word,
Each acted word,
wrapped in a miracle
of healing kindness.

I Practice Kindness

Tell me, pastor.
What is your day like?

I practice kindness.

If you learn of tragedy and death,
how do you respond?

I practice kindness.

If you go on vacation,
how do you act?

I practice kindness.

Bibliography

Aslan, Reza. *Zealot*. New York: Random House. 2013.

Aune, D. E. "The Apocalypse of John and Greco-Roman Revelatory Magic," *New Testament Studies*, 33. 1987.

_____. "The Form and Function of the Proclamation to the Seven Churches (Revelation 2-3)," *New Testament Studies*, 1990.

Barr, D. L. "The Apocalypse as a Symbolic Transformation of the World: A Literary Analysis," *Interpretation*. 38 (1984), 39-50.

Bauckham, Richard. *The Theology of the Book of Revelation*. New Testament Theology. Cambridge: Cambridge University Press, 1993.

Beale, G. K. *The Book of Revelation: A Commentary on the Greek Text*. The New International Greek Testament Commentary. Grand Rapids: Eerdmans, 2013.

Beasley-Murray, G. R. *The Book of Revelation*. New Century Bible. London: Marshal, Morgan & Scott, 1974.

Bernstein, Richard J. *Radical Evil: A Philosophical Interrogation*. Cambridge: Polity Press, 2002.

Boring, M. Eugene. *Revelation*. Interpretation. Louisville: John Knox, 1989.

Bracken, Joseph A. S.J. and Marjorie Hewitt Suchocki, ed. *Trinity in Process: A Relational Theology of God*. New York: Continuum Publishing Co., 1997.

Caird, G. B. *The Revelation of St. John the Divine.* Harper's New Testament Commentary. New York: Harper and Row. 1966.

Cobb, John B. Jr. *Becoming a Thinking Christian.* Nashville: Abingdon Press, 1993.

_____. *Christ In A Pluralistic Age.* Eugene, Or: Wipf and Stock Publishers, 1998.

_____. *Lay Theology.* St. Louis: Chalice Press, 1994.

Cole, Dwayne. *A Center that Holds: Adventures in Kindness.* Cleveland, Tennessee: Parson's Porch Books, 2015.

_____. *A Prayer of Blessing: As You Go Remember This.* Cleveland, Tennessee: Parson's Porch Books, 2015.

_____. *A Relational Trinity of Kindness.* Cleveland, Tennessee: Parson's Porch Books, 2015.

_____. *Jesus' Transforming Beatitudes: Selected Sermons from Year A.* Cleveland, Tennessee: Parson's Porch Books, 2015.

_____. *Jesus' Transforming Love: Selected Sermons from Year B.* Cleveland, Tennessee: Parson's Porch Books, 2014.

_____. *Jesus' Transforming Gentle Teachings: Selected Sermons from Year C.* Cleveland, Tennessee: Parson' Porch Books, 2015.

_____. *The Apostles' Creed: A Living Creed for the Living Church.* Cleveland, Tennessee: Parson's Porch Books, 2014.

_____. *The Book of Revelation: Jesus' Kindness Transforms Suffering.* Cleveland, Tennessee: Parson's Porch Books, 2015.

_____. *The Serenity Prayer: A Pathway to Peace and Happiness.* Cleveland, Tennessee: Parson's Porch Books, 2015.

_____. *The Story of the Bible: Authority, Inspiration, Canonization, and Translation.* Cleveland, Tennessee: Parson's Porch Books, 2015.

_____. "Taking the Pulse of the Universe," *The Cumberland Presbyterian Magazine,* January 2004.

_____. "Jesus Prays for the Church: Sermon Preached to the General Assembly of the Cumberland Presbyterian Church," *The Cumberland Presbyterian Magazine,* 1998.

_____. *Baptism and the Lord's Supper in the Gospel of John: A Hermeneutical Enquiry.* A Ph. D. dissertation at The Southern Baptist Theological Seminary, Louisville, Ky. 1973.

Daley, B. *The Hope of the Early Church.* Cambridge: Cambridge University Press, 1991.

Davis, Stephen T. Editor. *Encountering Evil: Live Options in Theodicy.* Atlanta: John Knox Press, 1981.

deSilva, David A. *Introducing the Apocalypse: Message, Context, and Significance.* Grand Rapids: Baker Academic. 2002.

Eagleton, Terry. *On Evil.* New Haven: Yale University Press, 2010.
Edwards, George R. *Jesus and the Politics of Violence.* New York: Harper & Row, 1972.

Ehrman, Bart D. *How Jesus Became God.* New York: Harper Collins Publishers, 2014.

Feuillet, A. *The Apocalypse*. Trans. T. E. Crane. New York: Alba House, 1965.

Ford, Lewis S. *The Lure of God: A Biblical Background for Process Theism*. Philadelphia: Fortress Press. 1978.

_____. *Transforming Process Theism*. Albany: State University Press. 2000.

Frank, Viktor E. *Man's Search for Meaning: An Introduction to Logotherapy*. Third Edition. New York: Simon & Schuster, 1984.

_____. *The Will to Meaning: Foundations and Applications of Logotherapy*. Expanded Edition. New York: Meridian, 1988.

Gregg, Steve. *Revelation: Four Views*. Revised and Updated. Nashville: Thomas Nelson, 2011.

Griffin, David R. *God, Power, and Evil: A Process Theodicy*. Philadelphia: The Westminster Press, 1976.

_____ and John B. Cobb. *Process Theology: An Introductory Exposition*. Philadelphia: The Westminster Press, 1976.

Hartshorne, Charles. *The Divine Relativity*. New Haven: Yale University Press, 1948.

Hicks, John H. *Evil and the God of Love*. New York: Harper & Row, 1977.

Jung, C. G. *Archetypes and the Collective Unconscious*. B. F. C. Hull, translator. Bollingen Series XX. Princeton University Press, 1969.

———. *Encountering Jung: On Evil.* Selected and Introduced by Murray Stein. Princeton: Princeton University Press. 1995.

Karr-Morse, Robin and Meredith S. Wiley. *Ghosts from the Nursery: Tracing the Roots of Violence.* New York: The Atlantic Monthly Press, 1997.

Kasemann, Ernst. *Jesus Means Freedom.* Translated by Frank Clarke. Philadelphia: Fortress Press, 1971.

Keller, Catherine. *On the Mystery: Discerning Divinity in Process.* Minneapolis Fortress Press, 2008.

Kidwell, Clara Sue, Homer Noley, and George E. *"Tink" Tinker. A Native American Theology.* New York: Orbis Books, 2001.

Levine, Any-Jill. *The Misunderstood Jew: The Church and the Scandal of the Jewish Jesus.* San Francisco: Harper, 2006.

———. *Short Stories by Jesus: The Enigmatic Parables of a Controversial Rabbi.* New York: Harper Collins, 2014.

McFague, Sallie. *Models of God.* Minneapolis: Augsburg Fortress, 1987.

———. *The Body of God: An Ecological Theology.* Minneapolis: Augsburg Fortress, 1993.

———. *Super, Natural Christians.* Minneapolis: Augsburg Fortress, 1997.

Medved, Michael and Diane Medved. *Saving Childhood: Protecting Our Children from the National Assault on Innocence.* New York: Harper Collins Publishers, 1998.

Murphy, R. "An Allusion to Mary in the Apocalypse," *Theological Studies*, 2:565-73, 1949.

Neiman, Susan. *Evil in Modern Thought: An Alternative History of Philosophy.* Princeton: Princeton University Press, 2002.

Pagels, Elaine. *Revelations: Visions, Prophecy, & Politics in the Book of Revelation.* New York: Penguin Group. 2012.

_____. *The Origin of Satan.* New York: Random House, 1995.
Parkin, David. *The Anthropology of Evil.* New York: Basil Blackwell, Inc., 1985.

Penny, Louise. *Kingdom of the Blind.* New York City: Minotaur Books, 2018.

Peterson, Michael L. Editor. *The Problem of Evil: Selected Readings.* Notre Dame, Indiana: University of Notre Dame Press, 1992.

Robben, Antonius C. G. M. and Marcelo M. Suarez-Orozco, eds. *Cultures under Seige: Collective Violence and Trauma.* Cambridge: Cambridge University Press, 2000.

Rowland, Christopher C. "The Book of Revelation." *The New Interpreter's* Bible, Vol. XII, Abingdon Press, 1998.

Salzberg, S. *Lovingkindness: The Revolutionary Art of Happiness.* Boston: Shambhala, 2002.

Schmithals, Walter. *The Apocalyptic Movement.* John E. Steely, editor. Nashville: Abingdon Press, 1975.

Snider, Tim. *All Things New: Understanding the Book of Revelation.* Bloomington: WestBow Press, 2011.

Suchocki, Marjorie Hewitt. *God Christ Church: A Practical Guide to Process Theology.* New Revised Edition. New York: The Crossroad Publishing Company, 1989.

_____. *The End of Evil: Process Eschatology in Historical Context.* Albany: State University, 1988.

_____. *In God's Presence: Theological Reflections on Prayer.* St. Louis: Chalice Press, 1996.

The Greek New Testament, Ed. Kurt Aland, Matthew Black, Carlo M. Martini, Bruce Metzger, and Allen Wikgren. Third Edition. United Bible Societies, 1975.

Thompson, Leonard L. *The Book of Revelation: Apocalypse and Empire.* New York: Oxford University Press. 1990.

Tobin, Thomas. "Logos," *The Anchor Bible Dictionary*, Vol. 4. New York: Doubleday, 1992.

Tournier, Paul. *The Violence Within.* Trans. Edwin Hudson. San Francisco: Harper & Row, 1978.

Wainwright, A. *Mysterious Apocalypse.* Nashville: Abingdon, 1993.

Whitehead, Alfred North. *Adventures of Ideas.* New York: The Free Press, 1967.

_____. *Process and Reality*. Corrected Edition, ed. David Ray Griffin and Donald W. Sherburne. New York: The Free Press, 1978.

_____. *Modes of Thought*. New York: The Free Press, 1968.

Wink, Walter. *Engaging the Powers: Discernment and Resistance in a World of Domination*. Minneapolis: Fortress Press, 1992.

_____. *Naming the Powers: The Language of Power in the New Testament*. Philadelphia: Fortress Press, 1984.

_____. *Unmasking the Powers: The Invisible Forces that Determine Human Existence*. Philadelphia: Fortress Press, 1986.

Woodruff, Paul and Harry A. Wilmer, Editors. *Facing Evil: Light at the Core of Darkness*. Lasalle, Illinois: Open Court Publishing Company, 1988.

Other Books by Dwayne Cole

A Center that Holds: Adventures in Kindness.

A Prayer of Blessing: As You Go Remember This.

A Relational Hermeneutic of Kindness.

A Relational Trinity of Kindness.

God and Evil: An Ode to Kindness.

Jesus' Transforming Beatitudes: Selected Sermons from Year A.

Jesus' Transforming Love: Selected Sermons from Year B.

Jesus' Transforming Gentle Teachings: Selected Sermons from Year C.

The Apostles' Creed: A Living Creed for the Living Church.

The Book of Revelation: Jesus' Kindness Transforms Suffering.

The Serenity Prayer: A Pathway to Peace and Happiness.

The Story of the Bible: Authority, Inspiration, Canonization, and Translation.

www.ingramcontent.com/pod-product-compliance
Lightning Source LLC
Chambersburg PA
CBHW052149110526
44591CB00012B/1913